LEGISLATING EQUALITY

Legislating Equality

*The Politics of Antidiscrimination
Policy in Europe*

TERRI E. GIVENS AND RHONDA EVANS CASE

OXFORD
UNIVERSITY PRESS

OXFORD

UNIVERSITY PRESS

Great Clarendon Street, Oxford, OX2 6DP,
United Kingdom

Oxford University Press is a department of the University of Oxford.
It furthers the University's objective of excellence in research, scholarship,
and education by publishing worldwide. Oxford is a registered trade mark of
Oxford University Press in the UK and in certain other countries

© Terri Givens and Rhonda Evans Case 2014

© Chapter 2 with Pete Mohanty 2014

The moral rights of the authors have been asserted

First Edition published in 2014

Impression: 1

Published in the United States of America by Oxford University Press
198 Madison Avenue, New York, NY 10016, United States of America

British Library Cataloguing in Publication Data
Data available

Library of Congress Control Number: 2013953567

ISBN 978-0-19-870901-5

Printed and bound by
CPI Group (UK) Ltd, Croydon, CR0 4YY

Dedicated to my boys, Mike, Andrew, and Brandon Scott

Acknowledgements

It is interesting to note that one of the key events from my 2005 book, *Voting Radical Right in Western Europe*, would launch the research for this book. The passage of the EU's Racial Equality Directive was a direct response to the 1999 Austrian legislative election, where the Austrian Freedom Party joined the government. At the time, I was surprised at how quickly the discourses around race and discrimination changed, leading me to investigate the background to these developments.

This book has been a project long in the making, and there are many people who helped along the way who I will not have the space to recognize, particularly the many undergraduates who spent a semester or two helping me do literature reviews, writing summaries, and following the news in Europe. I must begin by acknowledging, Rhonda Evans Case, who is a co-author on six of the chapters. Rhonda started working on this project with me early on as a research assistant and her legal background was very valuable for dealing with some of the legal complexities present in antidiscrimination law. She was also able to add to the research while conducting her own dissertation research in Europe. Much of her written contribution was done after she had become an assistant professor at East Carolina University. My graduate research assistant, Pete Mohanty, co-authored Chapter 2. He was very helpful with developing our quantitative approach to discursive institutionalism, the data analysis, and also helped with editing many of the other chapters.

One of the major influences on this book, and my research agenda overall, has been my colleague Gary Freeman. His influential work on immigration policy and immigrant integration was one of the inspirations for this book. Other influences include Jim Hollifield, Martin Schain, Anthony Messina, Dan Tichenor, Marc Rosenblum, Gallya Lahav, Andrew Geddes, Virginie Guiraudon, Daniel Sabbagh, Catherine De Wenden, and Riva Kastoryano. Along the way, I have been able to work with the new generation of scholars and appreciate the feedback I have received from Rahsaan Maxwell, Justin Gest, and some of my former students including Adam Luedtke and Christian Breunig. Special thanks to Rachel Navarre for her work on the index.

I conducted many interviews over the course of the research, and would like to thank in particular former MEP Glyn Ford, for not only providing his eyewitness account of the actions of the European Parliament, but also original documents and ultimately his hospitality in Brussels. I also received a great deal of information from the Migration Policy Group in Brussels, in particular from Jan Niessen and Isabelle Chopin. The staff of Equinet were very helpful, and I appreciate their allowing me to participate in their annual meetings, in particular Anne Gaspard, Tamas Kadar, Caroline Nsenda, and Yannick Godin.

During the main time period that I conducted the research for this book, I had support from the College of Liberal Arts at UT Austin, Fulbright, the German Marshall Fund, the Migration Policy Institute (particularly Natalia Banulescu-Bogdan, and intern Cristina Batog), the Kolleg-Forschergruppe "Transformative Power of Europe" Freie Universitaet, Berlin (thanks to Tanja Boerzel and Thomas Risse), and the Wilson Center in Washington, DC.

My husband Mike and two boys, Andrew and Brandon, regularly accompanied me on my research trips to Europe, and I thank them for their patience when I would have to leave them to their own devices in order to go to a meeting or conduct an interview. It is their love and support that kept me going during the good times and bad. Finally, I lost several family members, including my parents, over the last few years, and although they aren't here to see this book published, they are always with me in spirit, and I thank Rocelious and Leora Givens for the love and support that made me the person that I am.

Rhonda Evans Case thanks the Thomas Harriot College of Arts and Sciences at East Carolina University for the College Research Award that enabled her to undertake research for the book. She also thanks her colleagues in the Department of Political Science at East Carolina University for their support.

Contents

List of Tables and Figures

Tables

Figures

List of Abbreviations

ADRI	Agency for the Development of Intercultural Relations
AGG	*Allgemeines Gleichbehandlungsgesetz*
ARIC	Antiracist Information Centre
BDA	*Bundesvereinigung der deutschen Arbeitgeberverbände*
BDB	*Bund gegen ethnische Diskriminierung in der Bundesrepublik Deutschland*
BNP	British National Party
CDU	*Christlich Demokratische Union Deutschlands*
CEDRA	*Centre d'Etudes des Discriminations, du Racisme et de l'Antisémitisme*
CRE	Commission for Racial Equality
CRJ	Center for Juridical Resources
DGB	*Deutscher Gewerkschaftsbund*
DI	discursive institutionalism
DRC/DACoRD	Documentation and Advisory Centre on Racial Discrimination
DVU	German People's Union
ECJ	European Court of Justice
ECRI	European Commission against Racism and Intolerance
EFMS	European Forum for Migration Studies
EHRC	Equality and Human Rights Commission
ENAR	European Network against Racism
EP	European Parliament
ERRC	European Roma Rights Centre
ETDs	Equal Treatment Directives
EU	European Union
EUMC	European Monitoring Centre on Racism and Xenophobia
FDP	*Freie Demokratische Partei*
FPÖ	Freedom Party
FRA	Fundamental Rights Agency
GELD	*Groupe d'Etude et de Lutte contre les Discriminations*
HALDE	High Authority against Discrimination and for Equality
HI	historical institutionalism
ICERD	International Covenant on the Elimination of All Forms of Racial Discrimination
ICG	Intergovernmental Conference
ILGA	International Lesbian and Gay Association
FN	Front National

MEP	Member of the European Parliament
MPG	Migration Policy Group
MPI	Migration Policy Institute
MRAP	Movement against Racism and for Friendship among Peoples
MSI	*Movimento Sociale Italiano*
NF	National Front
NGOs	non-governmental organizations
NgR	*Netz gegen Rassismus*
NPD	*Nationaldemokratische Partei Deutschlands*
POS	political opportunity structure
PS	*Parti Socialiste*
RAXEN	European Information Network on Racism and Xenophobia
RCI	rational choice institutionalism
RED	Racial Equality Directive
REP	*Republikaner*
RPR	Rally for the Republic
SI	sociological institutionalism
SLG	Starting Line Group
SPD	*Sozialdemokratische Partei Deutschlands*
SVP	Swiss People's Party
TANs	transnational advocacy networks
TCNs	third-country nationals
TEC	Treaty Establishing the European Community
TEU	Treaty on European Union
UDHR	Universal Declaration of Human Rights
UKIP	United Kingdom Independence Party
UMP	*Union pour un Mouvement Populaire*
UN	United Nations
UNGA	United Nations General Assembly

1

Antidiscrimination Policy in an Integrating Europe*

1.1 INTRODUCTION

In October 1999 politicians around the European Union (EU) were stunned by the success of Jörg Haider's far right Freedom Party. When Haider's party became part of the Austrian government in early 2000, the other EU countries responded with diplomatic sanctions and within a few months would pass the Racial Equality Directive (RED), a measure that would require all 15 member states (and future members) to enact antidiscrimination policy into national law. Ten years later, despite some initial success with the development of national level equality bodies, many EU governments were slashing funding and moving once-independent entities into larger human rights bodies, thereby diluting their influence. The institutions created by the RED were under fire partly because of the ongoing fiscal crisis, but also due to political pressure. The RED and consequent Equal Employment and Gender Equality Directives (Equal Treatment Directives—2000/43/EC, 2004/113/EC, and 2006/54/EC) were a set of policies that developed along with European integration in the 1990s, but ran into the integration slowdown after enlargement in the mid-2000s, a fiscal crisis, and a lack of prioritization by mostly conservative governments.

Development of the Equal Treatment Directives (ETDs) closely mirrored European deepening in the 1990s, but its roots lie in events of the 1980s. Although European integration stalled during the 1980s, actors in the European Parliament (EP) saw a political opening for action with the rise of the radical right in places like France and Germany. In the 1980s and early 1990s, racist acts of violence and the stunning success of radical right political parties across Europe catapulted issues of immigration, xenophobia, fascism, and racism to the forefront. The European Parliament was only beginning to assume a more important place in the supranational structures that were under construction during the 1980s, but it would play a key role in the development of anti-racist and what would ultimately become racial antidiscrimination policy for the European Union. However, it is also important to note that the focus on anti-racism goes back to the civil rights era of the 1960s in the U.S. and the impact the American example had on policy in Europe, particularly in Great Britain.

Ethnic and racial discrimination has been an issue for Europe throughout history, but given issues of growing minority communities and anti-immigrant violence in Europe today, antidiscrimination policy would seem a natural area for concern. It is important to note that antidiscrimination policy did not develop directly from demands by minorities in these countries, as it did in the U.S. The development of legislation in the U.S. came during a time of great social upheaval in the 1960s. The situation in Europe was quite different. As a response to the rise of anti-immigrant radical right parties, politicians in Europe drew upon policies that diffused from North America to Great Britain in the late 1960s. This approach ultimately led to passage of the European Union's RED in 2000.

Beginning in 1965, Great Britain expressly recognized the role of race in its society because immigration from former colonies with diverse populations brought increasing numbers of ethnic minorities to its shores. Drawing upon the American example, Parliament enacted a series of laws that prohibited racial discrimination. It also established institutions specifically charged with their enforcement, including the Commission for Racial Equality (CRE). In important respects, the policies prescribed in the RED resemble these laws and institutions.

In the 1980s, increases in racist violence and entry of far right parties into the EP drew a response at the EU level. In 1984, the European Parliament took the lead in dealing with racial discrimination, led by a British Labour Party Member of the European Parliament (MEP), Glyn Ford. It was seen as, and certainly was at that time, a secondary institution, with little influence. However, it is clear that the actions taken by the EP in the mid-1980s set in motion a series of reports and actions that would ultimately lead to passage of the RED 20 years later. This book will explain how strategic actors (generally from the left) developed and used discourses to pass antidiscrimination legislation at the EU level. We then examine implementation of the legislation at the national level, describing the hurdles that legislative efforts faced as EU integration slowed and conservative parties came into government in many member states.

This book begins by examining the evolving discourses around racism in Europe from the mid-1980s through the late-1990s. We then link these discourses and national starting points to the political and social factors that influenced the development of antidiscrimination policy. We go on to explain why the European Parliament pursued an anti-racism agenda when it appeared to have no competence in this area and how anti-racism led to the development of antidiscrimination policy. Many of the ideas behind the EU's

RED undoubtedly came from early adopters of antidiscrimination policy, i.e., Britain and the Netherlands. But, how did these policy ideas develop in relation to European integration, and why were member states willing to pursue this policy agenda in light of very different national starting points? How did the development of antidiscrimination policy deviate from typical norms of policy development in the EU? What role did individuals and organizations play during the various processes that led to the passage of legislation?

The book goes on to examine the transposition of the EU Directives into national law and implementation of antidiscrimination policy. We argue that these processes were affected by the slowdown in European integration in the early 2000s as well as by political pressure from more conservative governments than those that had initially supported the legislation at the EU level.

1.1.1 The Main Puzzle and Argument

Why did antidiscrimination policy rise on the agenda for MEPs and ultimately EU member states? Violence against immigrants and ethnic minorities and racism emerged as important issues in the 1980s along with the rise of radical right parties, particularly when they entered the European Parliament in the 1984 election. Parties like the French National Front, led by Jean Marie Le Pen, held both anti-Semitic and anti-immigrant positions, and violence by skinheads and neo-Nazis increased during this time as well. These groups often linked economic issues, like unemployment, with the number of immigrants in their country, particularly immigrants from developing countries.

From an initial emphasis on anti-racism, actors at the EU level developed a series of discourses that were the building blocks for the EU's approach to racism and discrimination. Various actors used European institutions in strategic ways to bring these issues onto the agenda and helped to develop them into a concrete set of measures which became the Equality Directives. These Directives ran into a variety of issues when they had to be transposed at the national level, including a shift from left to right governments that often had little interest in supporting these measures.

The dependent variable in this analysis is the institutional response to various forms of racism and discrimination. These responses vary from in-depth reports and declarations, to antidiscrimination legislation and the creation of equality bodies. The independent variables include the presence of left-leaning parties or individuals in national governments and EU institutions, radical right violence or party success, developments in European integration, and changes in discourses around racism and discrimination. We develop the hypotheses to be tested through these variables in the theory section below.

European political elites grappled with three main policy questions, to which EU institutions, transnational human rights activists, and member states provided very different answers. The first issue was how to define the problem. Whereas member states preferred to define the problem narrowly in terms of hate speech and hate crimes, supra- and transnational actors defined the problem more broadly to include racial, ethnic, and religious discrimination. Second, who should take action to address the problem? Answers to this question derive from one's interpretation of who *could* take action. Supra- and transnational actors from non-governmental organizations (NGOs) sought to shift responsibility for this emerging policy area to the EU, claiming that the Union possessed competency to act under existing Treaty provisions. Although amenable to using supranational forums to denounce racism and xenophobia, member states rejected this claim and argued that European policy action could only proceed on the basis of a Treaty amendment.

Answers to these two questions shaped each actor's response to the final question—what policy action should be taken? Member states initially preferred intergovernmental cooperation and coordination of national policies against racist speech and violence, whereas the EP and transnational actors supported a European Directive that addressed racial discrimination in addition to racist speech and violence. During the 1990s a major shift occurred and member states like France and Germany began to support the development of a Treaty amendment that would allow the European Commission to develop racial antidiscrimination legislation.

> *The Puzzle*: How did racism get on the European Parliament's agenda? Why did the European Parliament pursue an anti-racism agenda when it had no competence in this area? How did anti-racism lead to the development of antidiscrimination policy?

Politicians and experts played a key role in developing the EU's approach to anti-racism and antidiscrimination policy by influencing the discourses through which the issues were defined. Prominent among them, Labour MEP Glyn Ford drew heavily from the British experience. The left dealt with the National Front and the British National Party, as well as racist immigration policies pursued by the Conservative Party in 1960s and 1970s, by pursuing "Race Relations" legislation that was designed to fight discrimination. This experience led to the approach taken by the EP in response to the rise of the radical right during the 1980s which revolved around an anti-racism discourse. This evolved to the discourses used by transnational actors like Jan Niessen in the 1990s who worked with the European Commission to push for antidiscrimination policy. After antidiscrimination policy was adopted by the left-leaning European Council in 2000, a general shift of conservative party electoral successes led to delays in adopting national level legislation and often weak implementation of the legislation. The discourses developed over the course of the 1980s and 1990s did not translate to the national level and in some cases were rejected as multiculturalism came under fire. Even after legislation was enacted, the public remained largely unaware of the role of these bodies and many of them had few staff to support their work. Equality bodies were negatively impacted by the fiscal crisis, and others were merged into larger human rights bodies that threatened to impact their effectiveness on specific discrimination issues.

We argue that two factors played an important role in the development of antidiscrimination policy in the EU. The first is racist anti-immigrant sentiment, and the second is left vs. right politics, i.e. the rise of the radical right as a catalyst for the passage of legislation and left support for antidiscrimination policy. However, these policy developments depended upon the process of Europeanization—as the European Union developed, political opportunities arose that allowed the issue of racism and antidiscrimination policy to move forward as a policy issue. Some, such as Geddes and Giraudon (2004, 2007), contend that the rise of the anti-immigrant Austrian Freedom Party catalyzed the passage of the EU's RED. Although this clearly had an impact, we show that the genesis of EU antidiscrimination policy goes back much further, to developments in the early 1980s. To understand these developments, they must be contextualized within the growth of discourses related to immigration and race in Europe, the evolving role of the European Parliament and the European Commission, and the strategic efforts of policy entrepreneurs to use these institutions to set the agenda and create the discourses around race and immigration that link the contemporary politics of hate to Europe's totalitarian past.

1.2 THEORY: HISTORICAL AND DISCURSIVE INSTITUTIONALISM

Because our analysis covers a broad swath of time and encompasses multiple variables, we use process tracing, a method favored by historical institutionalists who undertake longitudinal studies (Hall 1993: 292; Pierson 2003: 178). As Theda Skocpol (1995: 104) observes, this method is particularly well suited to inquiries that seek to "discover the intersections of separately structured developments that often account for outcomes we wish to understand." Process tracing allows the researcher to show how one event, policy, or process leads to the next. It shows how "patterns of resources and relationships in which individuals find themselves have powerful channeling and delimiting effects" and aims "to make those patterns visible and trace their causal impacts" (Pierson and Skocpol 2000: 7). Process tracing enables us to pay special attention to matters of timing and sequence (Pierson 2004) and to identify more complex causal patterns, as policies shape the contours of subsequent politics. Drawing on the framework of discursive institutionalism developed by Vivien Schmidt (Schmidt 2008), we examine how policy entrepreneurs were able to use institutions and ideas to introduce a new policy that would at least initially transform the way that many EU countries deal with issues of race and discrimination.

Our main hypothesis is that the increasing influence of left politics which favored minority rights vs. the anti-immigrant politics of the far right (which influenced the immigration control politics of the mainstream right) played an important role in the development of racial antidiscrimination policy as compared to gender discrimination which was based on concerns related to economic competition. However, it is not just at the level of parties that this difference played out: it was clearly at the level of individuals that this difference in approach played an important role. This argument is similar to that of Marc Morje Howard in his book on the politics of citizenship. Howard argues that change in citizenship policy is dependent upon the *politics* of citizenship. He states that "while citizenship liberalization is more likely to occur when the left is in power, the most important factor is the relative strength of far right parties, which can serve to mobilize latent anti-immigrant public opinion" (Howard 2009: 53). Our argument takes a somewhat different view, which is that *the strength of far right parties mobilized actors on the left who were able to take advantage of political institutions at the EU level to get race and discrimination onto the agenda.* Put differently, whereas Howard's unit of analysis is citizenship policy at the national level, we take a multilevel approach which focuses on the national and supranational contexts in which political actors on the left and right are relatively more or less powerful.[1]

We use the development of discourses over time to illustrate the shift in approach from anti-racism in the 1980s to antidiscrimination in the 1990s. We have conducted in-depth interviews with former members of the European Parliament and others who were involved with these issues from the 1980s through the passage of the EU RED in 2000, and on through the implementation of the Equality Directives and the 2010 review of the RED. Although we focus mainly on historical and discursive institutionalism for our analysis, some elements of rational choice institutionalism are incorporated into our analysis of the role of individual actors in the process of policy development.

1.2.1 Theory

We use a combination of institutionalist approaches in order to best explain the complex set of factors that led supranational actors to act to overcome the perceived inertia of national policies. Specifically, we draw on historical institutionalism to explain and analyze institutional preferences (for example, the European Commission's preference for further integration or the European Council's resistance to it) but it does not necessarily explain major shifts or the actions of agents that are involved in creating new institutional space. Rational choice institutionalism provides a structure for focusing on individual actors and their use of institutions to pursue a particular agenda: "relevant actors have a fixed set of preferences or tastes, behave instrumentally so as to maximize the attainment of these preferences" (Hall and Taylor 1996: 944–45). However, this approach does not help us to explain how shifting discourses shaped actors' preferences. Discursive institutionalism provides a framework that can take these factors into account including the discourses that provide the structure for change.

Combining primarily the framework of historical institutionalism with discursive institutionalism (Schmidt 2008, 2011) we seek to explain the factors that led policy-makers to emphasize first anti-racism and then racial antidiscrimination policy, and why the European Parliament and the Commission took on the issues before they possessed competence in these areas. We compare policies related to gender equality to the development of racial antidiscrimination policy to determine whether this represented a new approach to policy-making at the European Union level, in particular demonstrating the influence of policy networks.

The policy development process begins with the development of the Committee of Inquiry in the European Parliament that produced the Evrigenis Report in the 1980s, to the passage of the EU's RED by the late 1990s and implementation in the early 2000s. We divide the process into three time periods that roughly overlap the discourses adopted at the time (Table 1.1).

We combine analysis of primary and secondary documents with in-depth interviews with former members of the European Parliament and others who were involved with these issues from the 1980s through the passage of the EU RED in 2000 and up to the retrenchment on policy in the midst of the fiscal crisis in 2010:

- Members of Committees of Inquiry, including Chair, Glyn Ford
- Jan Niessen, Isabelle Chopin, and others from the Starting Line Group and Migration Policy Group
- European Commission Staff
- Equality body staff
- Stakeholders

These interviews provide support for the discourse analysis of primary documents from the 1980s and 1990s and help to elucidate the direction of negotiations and policy developments that led to the development of antidiscrimination policy in the European Union.

Table 1.1 Three European discourses about discrimination policy

	1980s	1990s	2000s
Discourse	Discourse I: Anti-racism	Discourse II: Antidiscrimination	Implementation and rejection of prior discourses
Logic	Extremism suggests resurgence of Europe's totalitarian past	Individuals have certain rights regardless of motives of discriminator	Retrenchment of EU mandates; multiculturalism threatens national unity; emphasis on immigrant responsibilities, not rights
Policy archetype	British race relations policy, U.S. civil rights	Britain, Belgium, and Netherlands Anti-Discrimination Policy	Immigrant civic integration, particularly in Germany and Netherlands
Motivating events	Rise of radical right, violence against immigrants	Ongoing radical right success (particularly Austrian Freedom Party), rising supranationalism	Slowdown in European integration caused by expansion, economic downturn, fiscal crisis
Proponents	Glyn Ford	Kohl and Mitterand, transnational activists, Jan Niessen	Conservative governments (particularly France and Germany)
Opponents	European Council (member states)	Domestic opponents of supranational legislation	Transnational activists

1.3 LITERATURE REVIEW

The literature on comparative antidiscrimination policy is nascent in political science. As the topic of immigration becomes of greater interest (e.g., the formation of an immigration section in the American Political Science Association in 2012) the situation of immigrant communities and integration has also come to the fore. However, relatively few in-depth studies exist at this point. We begin with a review of different approaches that have been used to analyze the intersection of immigration, race, and discrimination in Europe. We then briefly examine the debate between intergovernmentalist and supranational theorists and the role of the European Parliament. The role of transnational actors is an important aspect of our analysis, and we combine our examination of that literature with an assessment of the role of left and right politicians within the context of the EU institutions.

Two important books examine how European countries have responded to the influx of millions of "non-white" immigrants since World War II. Focusing on Great Britain and France, Bleich (2003) emphasizes the role of ideas in policy development. He argues that differences in the race policies of France and Great Britain are best explained by differences in the way in which race has historically been "framed" in each country. In Britain, race policy reflects a multicultural approach that frames racism in terms of color and identifies with problems of racism in North America. By contrast, in France the frame derives the country's experiences with anti-Semitism rather than any comparison with North American issues. Although we acknowledge that ideas shape political discourse and thus influence policy development, like Lieberman (2005), we do not believe that ideas alone offer a complete explanation.

Lieberman (2005) emphasizes the interplay of ideas and political institutions in his study of welfare and antidiscrimination policies in the U.S., Great Britain, and France. Focusing on immigrant incorporation through antidiscrimination policy, he compares race-conscious affirmative action in the U.S. to "race relations" in Britain, and to color-blind policies in France. Despite the weakness of the American state apparatus, Lieberman finds that antidiscrimination efforts in the U.S. were much stronger than those in France and Britain with their more centralized states. He concludes that neither state structure nor "ideas and cultural dispositions by themselves" explain political and policy outcomes. This is especially true "in race policy, which generally involves conflict and contestation among competing ideas—particularly between varieties of race consciousness and color blindness... Ideas, in short, give us motive but not opportunity" (Lieberman 2005: 11). Lieberman contends that political institutions and competition shape the development of race policy. Policy-making, he notes, "entails the formation of coalitions among actors who represent both interests vying for power and diverse policy ideas" (Lieberman 2005: 12). Therefore, one must understand the interplay between ideological and cultural traditions in relation to state structures as well as the "capacity of groups to mobilize and use those institutions as leverage to further their particular policy visions" (Lieberman 2005: 200).

1.3.1 Theories of European Integration

Particularly in the 1990s, scholars used three main approaches to understand European integration: neofunctionalism, intergovernmentalism, and supranationalism. According to intergovernmentalists, member states play a key role in constructing ideas and disseminating them to the EU. Neofunctionalism, as formulated by Ernst Haas and Leon Lindberg, describes EU integration as a movement toward political integration while emphasizing the process by which group pressures cause loyalties to shift toward a new center, with the end result being the creation of a new political community. As Haas argued, "Political integration is the process whereby political actors in several distinct national settings are persuaded to shift their loyalties, expectations, and political activities toward a new centre, whose institutions possess or demand jurisdiction over the pre-existing national states" (Haas 1958: 16).

In terms of policy-making, neofunctionalism as a theoretical lens would posit an increase over time in the salience of supranational institutions. Therefore, one would see the development of the European Council and Commission as the main decision-making bodies that drive policy in the European Union. As the supranational body undertakes more and more tasks, new policy arenas come under its purview and are incorporated into the supranational mechanism.

Intergovernmentalism grew out of a realist approach to European integration. Stacey points out that "According to Intergovernmentalism, EU Member States generally not only prefer to retain their sovereignty, but they also possess the ability to prevent the transfer of sovereignty to supranational organizational actors whenever they wish to exercise it" (Stacey 2010: 7). Proponents of this theory argue that the institutional setup of the European Commission and therefore its policy-making mechanisms are the product of a conscious strategy by the member states. Policy-making within the European Union according to the intergovernmentalism school is therefore the result of a compromise between the member states to keep the supranational body they have designed, the Commission, in check. The member states agree to keep the Commission in line with their interests through a number of checks and balances, from veto powers on certain issues (such as those that fell within the Third Pillar of the EC Treaty or that concern the Common Foreign and Security Policy) to regulatory decisions undertaken through the Comitology procedure. The advent of Comitology, a system of committees set up to monitor regulatory decisions made by the Commission, itself was an answer to the question of how the Council could exert control over the Commission and prevent "bureaucratic drift." As Ballmann et al. argue, "Legislative bodies often limit drift by establishing specialized committees and subcommittees which work as a sort of fire alarm system" (Ballmann et al. 2002: 555).

Ultimately, in the intergovernmentalist theory, most policy is derived through bargaining between the main centers of power; they build coalitions and alliances on various issues and then push them through the EU supranational level. These initial interests, however, are posited at the domestic politics level. Domestic politics is inherently an extension of the rational choice paradigm. Intergovernmentalism places great emphasis on domestic politics and as posited by Andrew Moravscik: "States (or other political institutions) represent some subset of domestic society, on the basis of whose interests state officials define state preferences and act purposively in world politics" (Moravscik 1997: 518). Policy-making in the EU may therefore be negotiated at the supranational level through intergovernmental methods, but interests are defined on the national level.

Supranationalism or supranational governance theory developed as a way to explain increased European integration in the 1990s which could not be explained by liberal intergovernmentalism. Stacey refers to this development as a "reformulation of neofunctionalism" (Stacey 2010: 12). Neofunctionalism was unable to account for the lack of progress in European integration in the 1980s, and fell out of favor as a theory. By the late 1990s, it was becoming clear that deeper integration would lead to new powers for institutions like the European Commission and the European Court of Justice (ECJ). Stacey notes that the proponents of this theory argue that "existing rules motivate supranational actors not only to exploit them but also to create new rules of their own accord—and expand their organizational capacity in the process" (Stacey 2010: 13). Stacey also notes that this argument is basically tautological, since the Commission has also to work with "and bargain with a council that vigorously defends it prerogatives" (Stacey 2010: 13). European institutions are some of the key players in our analysis, including the European Parliament.

The European Parliament was often seen as a weak player within the array of European institutions, particularly by intergovernmentalists. However, authors such as Tsebelis saw the role of the EP in a different light: the EP could be a strategic player. In his seminal 1994 article, "The Power of the European Parliament as a Conditional Agenda Setter," Tsebelis shows that the EP could make use of elements of its institutional design to go beyond typical areas of competence. As we will show, this was clearly the case when the EP began to examine issues of racism in the 1980s. Stacey (2010) challenges liberal intergovernmentalism with his emphasis on the role of informal rules in the development of policy in the EU. His analysis indicates that the political opportunism of the European Parliament often led to policy changes that would ultimately become part of major treaties, as with the focus on antidiscrimination policy in the 1980s and 1990s.

1.3.2 The Role of Transnational Actors

In October 1997, member states agreed to add Article 13 to the Treaty on European Union (TEU), thereby giving the EU authority to act with regard to discrimination on grounds of race, and less than three years later they enacted the RED. Article 13 and the RED constitute distinct steps in the Europeanization of racial antidiscrimination policy. In accordance with liberal intergovernmentalism, member states were the primary agents of change, and it attributes their behavior to a desire to strengthen, rather than weaken, "their control over domestic affairs" (Moravcsik 1993: 507). Member states, the argument goes, sought to Europeanize racial antidiscrimination policy in reaction to electoral gains made by radical right political parties and rising rates of racist and xenophobic violence. Scholars who endorse this account note that key policy actions taken by the Council of Ministers coincided with radical right gains (Wallace 2000; Geddes and Guiraudon 2002; Bell 2002). In explaining the passage of Article 13, they attribute special significance to a 1994 Franco-German initiative that established the European Consultative Commission on Racism and Xenophobia, also known as the "Kahn Commission" after its chair, Jean Kahn, head of the European section of the World Jewish Congress. This Commission was established during a period in which the radical right was increasingly assertive. It ultimately recommended that the Treaty of Amsterdam be amended to assign the EU competency over racial antidiscrimination policy.

The Council adopted the RED in July 2000—just seven months after the Commission released its proposal. Scholars suggest that in doing so member states were reacting to the success of Jörg Haider's anti-immigrant Freedom Party (FPÖ) at Austria's 1999 parliamentary election and its subsequent entry into a coalition government in February 2000 (Bell 2002; Geddes and Guiraudon 2004). Focusing only on the rise of the radical right, however, offers an "ex post" account of member state preferences that preserves "the image of near total member state control" (Pierson 1996: 125). Doing so illustrates a key weakness of liberal intergovernmental theory which focuses on the national level, while we argue that events at the transnational level were just as important in the development of this legislation. This brings us to the second explanation, the transnational advocacy thesis.

According to Keck and Sikkink (1998), "transnational advocacy networks" (TANs) are networks of activists who share a common set of values and beliefs, and can act as critical agents of policy and political change. These networks tend to be most effective in mobilizing around issues that concern "legal equality of opportunity" (Keck and Sikkink 1998: 27), precisely the sort of issue involved here. They usually exert influence in two ways. First, they "gain leverage over much more powerful organizations and governments" by altering "the information and value context within which states make policies" (Keck and Sikkink 1999: 89, 95). Second, TANs engage in "accountability politics," in other words, they shame governments into compliance by eliciting from them public commitments to particular human rights principles and then using information "to expose the distance between discourse and practice" (Keck and Sikkink 1998: 98). TANs insert a greater degree of agency into neofunctionalist theories that emphasize the role of "spillover" in the process of European integration (Haas 1958: Lindberg 1963).

Scholars readily acknowledge the important role played by the Starting Line Group (SLG) (Bell 2002; Chalmers 2000a; Geddes 2000), a transnational advocacy network that emerged in 1991 with the sole objective of obtaining an EU racial antidiscrimination Directive. None, however, has fully explained the SLG's role and evaluated its performance with regard to Article 13 and the RED. Those who subscribe to liberal intergovernmental explanations for European integration acknowledge the SLG's lobbying efforts, but they discount the network's influence because its representatives were not physically present at the RED's negotiations (Tyson 2001). Our analysis shows that their physical presence was not required.

As Keck and Sikkink (1998: 12) observe, "geographic distance, the influence of nationalism, the multiplicity of languages and cultures, and the costs of fax, phone, mail, and air travel" all conspire to render international networking a costly enterprise. All of these factors, as well as a deep suspicion concerning the EU among many activists, existed at the dawn of the 1990s, as Ann Dummett, a part-time consultant on European issues for Britain's Commission for Racial Equality, recounted in a 1991 article (Dummett 1991). How then was the SLG able to develop into an influential transnational advocacy network capable of successfully campaigning for EU racial antidiscrimination laws? First, the rubric of antidiscrimination law provided a discursive vocabulary that emphasized equality and thus fit well with the values of pro-migrant groups. It also served as a focal point for the coordination of an otherwise disparate array of organizations. Second, the European Commission, which was looking to partner with NGOs in order to advance the social dimension of the EU, helped the SLG overcome its resource constraints. Finally, because lawyers played such a critical role in the network, the SLG was able to exploit the Commission's role as a "process manager" (Eichener 1993), coordinating the "dense networks of experts" that are instrumental to the EU's regulatory style of policy-making (Pierson 1996: 133).

However, it is also clear that the RED could not have been passed without the support of left politicians. The left needed supranationalism to implement their policy agenda which, in fact, was a set of policies that would mean a great deal of change at the national level for countries like France and Germany. TANs helped lay the groundwork for the RED in the 1990s, after the initial infrastructure for action at the EU level had been laid through the actions of politicians in the European Parliament, like Glyn Ford.

However, once the RED was being transposed, many of the governments had shifted to right parties (particularly France and Germany). In a process not entirely dissimilar to the challenges the United States federal government faced when it was forced to rely upon the states to enforce key elements of civil rights law, intergovernmentalism became the "Achilles' heel" of implementation. The politics of transposition was fraught, with countries taking longer than the required three years to transpose the Directives into law. Once they were passed by national parliaments, implementation was uneven at best, particularly for the development of equality bodies that already existed in some countries but not in others. We will examine the implementation of the Equality Directives at the national level and discuss the impact of national level politics once these initiatives became law.

1.4 DEVELOPING THE ANALYSIS

In order to examine the development of antidiscrimination policy from the 1980s through 2010, we focus on three time periods: the 1980s, 1990s, and 2000–2011. The first step is the discourse analysis in Chapter 2, which looks at the development of key discourses around anti-racism and discrimination through the passage of the RED in 1999. Throughout our analysis, we examine the role of institutional structures like the European Parliament, European Commission, and European Council. Perhaps the most important aspect of the institutional analysis is the major institutional changes linked to European integration from the early 1980s through 1999. As EU institutions like the Parliament and Commission saw their areas of competence increase, they were able to take action in matters like immigration and antidiscrimination policy. However, they also found ways to influence the agenda, such as the European Parliament's use of Committees of Inquiry. NGOs and activists were able to use their increasing access to the European Commission to make proposals that would lead to the development of a draft Directive. Finally, the European Commission would immediately use its expanded competence under the Amsterdam Treaty to pursue the passage of the RED. The institutional structures are only one part of the story, and we also examine, through process tracing, the actions of particular actors and their impact on policy development during different time periods.

After analyzing developments at the EU level, the study moves to the national level from 2000 through 2010. Although the Equality Directives have been transposed in nearly all EU countries, in examining implementation we focus our analysis on France, Germany, and Britain. We do so for several reasons. These three countries have dominated policy-making at the EU level, particularly at the seminal moment of the negotiations of the Maastricht Treaty (Moravcsik 1998). Further, they are the "policy entrepreneurs" on most significant policy initiatives in the EU or at least significant players whose opposition has to be bridged before progress is made. For the purposes of research on immigration and discrimination, France, Germany, and Britian are also countries whose immigration policies most affected discourses on European immigration and citizenship rights. And finally, the three received overwhelmingly more immigrants since World War II than any other countries in Europe.

France, Germany, and Britain have transposed the RED, although to varying degrees and at varying rates of speed. Table 1.2 describes the steps each country has taken toward transposition and implementation of the RED. Member states were required to transpose the Directive's terms into national law by July 2003. Only France, however, reported to the Commission that it had made progress toward transposition by this deadline. Since then, Britain—out of our three cases—has moved the furthest in transposing and implementing the

Table 1.2 Transposition of the EU's Racial Equality Directive in Britain, Germany, and France

RED transposition overview	Legislation enacted to implement provisions under RED, to make discrimination illegal	Has instituted an equality body to issue sanctions and implemented provisions of RED	Application of RED and sanctions issued from 2005–2006
Britain	Equality Act 2006	Equality Act establishes Commission for Equality and Human Rights	Sanctions under RED legislation are considerable and occur often[a]
France	• Racial Equality Directive Law, adopted Dec. 31, 2004 • Employment Framework Directive, adopted Dec. 31, 2004 • Law creating an "equality body," adopted April 2, 2006	*La haute autorité de lutte contre les discriminations et pour l'égalité* (law of Apr. 2, 2006) (High authority for fight against discrimination and for equality)	Sanctions under RED legislation are considerable and occur often[b]
Germany	Law from Aug. 14, 2006: *Allgemeines Gleichbehandlungsgesetz* (AGG) (General law on equal treatment)	*Antidiskriminierungsstelle des Bundes* (Federal antidiscrimination office) established Oct. 1, 2006	No data available

[a] In 2005: 1,028 complaints of racial/ethnic discrimination received by specialized body; 119 employment discrimination cases brought to employment tribunals; 73 sanctions for racial/ethnic discrimination issued by employment tribunals, median award (9,859 euros), average award (45,079 euros), maximum award (1,461,995 euros).
[b] Between March 2005 and February 2006: 729 complains of racial/ethnic discrimination received by the specialized body; 12 sanctions for racial/ethnic discrimination issued by specialized body (only for 2005); average sanction 1,270 euros.

Directive. By 2004, France had enacted laws comparable to those of Britain. France's President Nicolas Sarkozy has also focused on the issue of "positive discrimination" similar to affirmative action in the United States. Finally, Germany managed to transpose the RED in 2006 (not the last country from the EU-15 to do so, but close).

In addition, Britain, France, and Germany provide important variations in terms of their antidiscrimination policies and national institutional structures. Britain is governed by a semi-centralized parliamentary governmental structure, led by a Prime Minister. France, by contrast, is highly centralized and has a dual executive, led by both a Prime Minister and a President. Germany is a federal system, with a parliamentary structure led by a Chancellor. As we will show, these institutional differences play a role in structuring both politics and policy development. The politics engendered by Germany's institutional structure slowed the passage of legislation related to transposition of the RED, while France and Britain's more centralized institutions allowed for quicker passage of such legislation, although these institutions did not necessarily facilitate quick implementation.

1.5 CONCLUSION AND CHAPTER OUTLINE

This book will cover 35 years of history, a period of time when the European Union and its nation states were going through major changes in terms of European integration. Through this analysis we will provide a unique perspective on legislative processes at the EU level. Often the development of EU Directives is an opaque process, and the role of actors like the European Parliament is considered minimal in comparison to the European Commission. This analysis brings the role of the EP to light at a time when it was considered a junior partner of the European institutions.

The development of the Equality Directives traces a period of deepening integration and the shift from being an economic trade union to a social and political union. We start in Chapter 2 with an analysis of the discourses that led to the passage of the EU's RED. Chapter 3 provides background on the status of antidiscrimination policy at the national level prior to the passage of the Equality Directives, to provide context for the positions taken by key players leading up to the passage of the RED in 2000. We then go on in Chapter 4 to examine in detail the events during the 1980s leading up to the development of an anti-racism agenda in the European Parliament, focusing on the role of key players and the discourses they used to define the problem. Chapter 5 focuses on the 1990s, when there was a shift in the European Council that ultimately led to Article 13 of the Amsterdam Treaty which opened the door to legislation on antidiscrimination policy. The actual passage of the RED and Equal Employment Directives are detailed in Chapter 6. At this point we turn to the national level analysis, examining the transposition of the RED in Chapter 7 and the retrenchment that occurred in most countries during the mid-to-late 2000s. Chapter 8 concludes with an examination of the future of antidiscrimination policy in Europe in light of the experience in the United States.

NOTES

*   This chapter was written with Rhonda Evans Case.

1. For more on the EU as a multilevel institution, see, for example, Hooghe and Marks (2001).

2

Analyzing Discourses[*]

2.1 INTRODUCTION

As discussed in Chapter 1, the broad framework of this analysis will be an institutionalist approach, drawing on three variants: historical, rational choice, and discursive institutionalism. The main focus of this chapter will be text analysis, but we begin by examining some of the issues surrounding the development of antidiscrimination policy.

One of the main arguments in this book is that the rise of radical right parties and the response by the left in the 1980s and 1990s were the main catalyst for the development of what ultimately would become antidiscrimination policy. This policy was reached through a series of developments, beginning with the European Parliament's first Committee of Inquiry which resulted in the Evrigenis Report of 1986. We also argue, however, that the development of the discourses around antidiscrimination policy was influenced by the British approach to "race relations" which was brought into the European Parliament by British MEP Glyn Ford who chaired the first Committee of Inquiry and was the rapporteur for the second Parliament Committee of Inquiry which resulted in the Ford Report in 1991.

As the governments of France and Germany pushed for deeper political integration of the EU, they called for the creation of a Council-level Commission to explore the issue of racism in Europe. The Kahn Commission produced a report which began to shift the discourse from anti-racism to an approach that would incorporate antidiscrimination policy. At the same time, the Starting Line Group was also beginning to pursue antidiscrimination policy through the European Commission. When the Amsterdam Treaty allowed the Commission to propose legislation in the area of antidiscrimination, it already had a draft Directive to build on. Then, with the Austrian parliamentary election of 1999, the Commission was able to present the draft Directive as a response to the entry of the far-right Freedom Party into the Austrian government. The result was the passage of the Racial Equality Directive in 2000.

As we describe below, we develop a quantitative analysis which allows us to compare the development of these discourses over time. Analyzing the discourses in various documents allows us to track the development of strategies and ultimately policy used by actors at the EU level. These actors were using both the discourses we analyze in this chapter and institutions to move forward an agenda that member states were not necessarily supporting.

2.2 POLITICAL OPPORTUNITY STRUCTURE AND INSTITUTIONALISM

One basic way to approach the development of antidiscrimination policy in Europe is through shifts in the political opportunity structure (POS). We draw on Koopmans' critique of social movement analyses which use the POS framework:

> The idea of political opportunity structure involves not more (and not less) than the claim that not all of the variation in levels and forms of collective action is due to the strategic wit, courage, imagination, or plain luck (or the lack of those) of the different actors involved in conflict situations, but that an important part of it is shaped by structural characteristics of the political context in which social movements, willingly or unwillingly, have to act. The relative extent to which structure and agency contribute to the explanation of such variation will undoubtedly vary from case to case and is, again, a matter for empirical investigation. (Koopmans 1999: 100)

A POS approach is normally used to examine social movements and conflict, but in this case it allows us to understand the interaction between specific actors and the changing institutions of the European Community in the 1990s, as integration increased. However, POS does not provide a complete framework for understanding the development of policy over time at the EU level.

The main frameworks used in this analysis—historical, rational choice, and discursive institutionalism—allow us to take an analytical approach to the development of political opportunities that arose at particular moments in time. Process tracing allows us to pinpoint the time periods when the political opportunity structure was open for political entrepreneurs to take advantage of the structures in place. Rational choice institutionalism helps to explain the rationale behind the choices made by political entrepreneurs. Discursive institutionalism lays out the discourses and "frames" that determine the direction of policy-related actions.

Ideas often serve as the tether between institutions and interests because partisans must be able to communicate their agenda to a broad public and to coordinate narrow policy details with elite actors. Discursive institutionalism (DI) is an approach which focuses on the role ideas play creating and transforming interests and institutions. DI builds on the existing frameworks of historical institutionalism (HI), sociological institutionalism (SI), and rational choice institutionalism (RCI) by providing a method which is sensitive to both context and agency.[1] This chapter analyzes the evolution of the communicative and coordinative dimensions of political ideas that led to the development of the RED.

In order to examine the development of antidiscrimination policy in the European context, this book draws heavily on the work of Vivien Schmidt on European integration. Schmidt has developed the framework of discursive institutionalism in order to develop models that allow for the role of discourses in the context of policy development. Our analysis builds on this by adding a quantitative component to the study of discourses, using word counts and data analysis to show the development of discourses around anti-racism and antidiscrimination policy over time.

2.3 DISCURSIVE INSTITUTIONALISM AS QUALITATIVE APPROACH

The RED has been described as a major shift in the development of policy, but the change occurred over a period of time when the types of discourses related to these issues shifted from a focus on the radical right and anti-racism to the issue of third-country nationals (TCNs) and antidiscrimination policy. In this section, we examine this shift through the tool of text analysis.

Discursive institutionalism is "an umbrella concept for the vast range of works in political science that take into account the substantive content of ideas and the interactive processes that serve to generate those ideas and communicate them to the public" (Schmidt 2011: 47). Political actors, particularly political parties, must be able to link broad public philosophies with narrow policy solutions. Political actors seek to define problems in a way that bridges principles which are generally held by some segment of the population and their particular agenda. This framing establishes a narrative: symptoms, disease, and remedy; antagonists and protagonists (see Table 2.1).

Framing homelessness as a personal failing makes it easier to defend government inaction because, according to this rationale, helping the homeless will not get to the root of the issue (laziness, addiction, etc.) and may even make the problem worse (by encouraging flawed behavior). Regardless of their intentions, those supporting the Federal Housing Authority thereby become "part of the problem," much the same way the loved one of an alcoholic may inadvertently "enable" the disease in an attempt to support the afflicted. Defining the social phenomena in this way links a modern

Table 2.1 Competing responses to homelessness

Scope	Idea type	Example	Idea role
Broad	Public philosophies	Laissez-faire vs. Keynesianism	
			Communicative
	Problem definitions	Homelessness: personal failing or housing shortage?	
Narrow	Policy solutions	No government action vs. Federal Housing Authority	*Coordinative*

problem to longstanding notions of individual responsibility, which thus provides a moral rationale for adopting a laissez-faire economic response. Conversely, defining homelessness as the result of a housing shortage suggests that, even if certain groups are disproportionately affected, it basically "could have happened to anyone." Therefore, according to this discourse, the root of the problem is a morally arbitrary market shortcoming and there is no reason not to remedy it (with the FHA or, more broadly, Keynesianism). Defining homelessness in these economic terms thus reinforces arguments which might be made based on notions of collective responsibility and the common good.

Which ideas prevail? DI focuses on: (1) power and resources of claimants, (2) issue framing, (3) venue in which debate is heard, (4) issue ownership, (5) available policy solutions (*coordinative* role), and (6) fit with broader environment (*communicative* role) (Mehta 2011: 35). By focusing on such elements as the power and resources of claimants and choice of venue, DI encourages scholars to focus on the strategic nature of political communication (much like RCI). By focusing on issue framing and ownership as well as the fit between the policy and the wider political environment, DI encourages scholars to focus on the ideas and institutions (much like HI and SI). Separating these elements also highlights differences in their rates of change: though it is punctuated by elections, the broader political environment generally changes more slowly than other factors such as framing or policy options. We lay out the competing ideas used to frame responses to hate crimes in Table 2.2.

Discursive institutionalism provides researchers with the necessary tools to analyze political ideas succinctly and methodically. The focus on Nazism, fascism, and extremism of the 1980s (Evrigenis and Ford reports) may have been effective *communicatively*, i.e., at communicating general concern to parties and to the public, but it was less effective *coordinatively*, in that this discourse did not imply clear, narrow policy goals. Banning extremist

Table 2.2 Competing responses to hate crimes in Europe

Scope	Idea type	Example	Idea role
Broad ↑	Public philosophies	Antifascism vs. multiculturalism	
			Communicative
	Problem definitions	Hate crimes: neo-Nazism or discrimination?	
Narrow ↓	Policy solutions	Anti-discrimination law	*Coordinative*

Table 2.3 Which ideas prevail?

Power and resources of claimants	Importance of NGOs in compensating for political disorganization of victims of hate crimes; paucity of elected radical right politicians
Issue framing	Hate crimes: neo-Nazism or discrimination?
Venue in which debate is heard	Necessity of expanded EU competence (RED would not have been possible on country-by-country basis)
Issue ownership	Left owned anti-discrimination
Available policy solutions (*coordinative* role)	Existing member state equality law, particularly that of the UK
Fit with broader environment (*communicative* role)	Coincidence of anti-discrimination agenda with goals of deepened and widened EU; fear of rising radical right

political activity or hate speech arguably would have done little to combat the wide variety of discrimination that minorities faced in Europe on a daily basis. The rise of the discourse on discrimination helped elite actors coordinate the proposed Racial Equality Directive with existing antidiscrimination law regarding gender and, in certain member states, race and ethnicity. The timing of the passage of the Directive, however, shortly after the election of Jörg Haider, shows that proponents of the RED still needed the anti-fascist discourse to overcome the political inertia necessary to legitimate an expansion area of EU lawmaking competence. Changing the venue not only favored one side, it ultimately changed the power of the venue itself. Different factors influencing the way ideas may influence outcomes are laid out in Table 2.3.

2.4 DISCURSIVE INSTITUTIONALISM AS QUANTITATIVE APPROACH

Quantitative methods can reinforce qualitative findings. In this section, we show step-by-step how to demonstrate changes in discursive emphasis (Neuendorf 2002).

> *Step 1*: *Identify key documents.* This step is arguably the most crucial. No method can make an argument persuasive when the data are of poor quality or irrelevant. What type of document is most relevant will depend on the scope of the idea under investigation and the hypotheses being advanced. Public philosophies may, for example, be well analyzed through media documents, partisan problem definitions through party platforms, and policy solutions through position papers and legislative documents. In our case, our choice of documents was also informed by elite interviews. The documents we analyze are:
>
> - The European Parliament's Evrigenis Report (1986)
> - The European Parliament's Ford Report (1991)
> - The Kahn Commission Report (1996)
> - The European Parliament EU Anti-Discrimination Policy Working Document (1997)
> - The Racial Equality Directive (2000)
>
> *Step 2*: *Identify key concepts.* The hardest part of choosing concepts is *not deciding whether* some concept (say, nationalism) is relevant to the debate (which is usually quite clear from reading the document), but choosing *how many gradations* of a concept are relevant. On the one hand, umbrella concepts obfuscate important dynamics. For example, if we had defined "discrimination" to include all references to Nazism, racism, xenophobia, and so on, we would not be able to show the dramatic increase in emphasis on the former at the expense of the latter. On the other hand, defining concepts so precisely that they are barely distinguishable from particular words introduces a bias toward concepts that can be expressed one, and only one, way. For example, "anti-Semitism," "anti-Judaism," and "anti-Zionism" are slightly different things, but if we had not combined them, we would have made "anti-Semitism" look (relatively) underemphasized. Thus, identifying key concepts is not the same as identifying different parts of speech. Software is available that will combine, for instance, "racism" and "racist" automatically, but only the researcher can decide whether two narrow concepts should be combined into a wider one. When in doubt, code the narrow concepts first and combine them later if it does not lead to loss of meaning (we combined "Nazism," "Fascism," and "Totalitarianism" into "Europe's Totalitarian Past" in this way).[2]

Step 3: Generate word counts. The next step is to generate a breakdown of all words occurring in the document(s). Documents must be in a text format before they are analyzed (that is, they cannot be scanned images). We used ABBYY software to convert image documents into text. Next, we generated word counts using Yoshikoder.[3] Generating word counts for all documents at once is preferable because the output allows for easy, side-by-side comparison of documents (if this is not an option, outputted word counts should be combined such that there is a column for each document and a row for each word).

Step 4: Classify. Next, the researcher should classify each of the words by key concept. Since there are multiple ways to refer to any given concept, researchers must create a "dictionary" which contains all of the relevant references (or find an existing one for that topic). For example, the words "racist" and "racism" both refer to racism. When working in Excel, this can be done simply by creating a column, entering a code for each key concept, and then using the "sumif" function elsewhere on the spreadsheet to generate word totals.

Step 5: Verify. Measurement error is part of the measurement process but whether the measurement error contained in any given coding is tolerable will depend on the word in question. We spot-checked each of the references to make sure we were not overlooking unusual usages. For example, in the texts we examined, "race" and related parts of speech always refer to the discussion of racism (and not to the arms race, dog racing, or any other type of race). The word "right," however, was used to refer to legal rights, to rightist political actors, and to correctness. Because of the variety of legal rights found in the text (free speech, fair trial, asylum, and so on) and the possibility that multiple senses of "right" would appear inside a sentence, it is not clear that software which searched for phrases would improve matters much. Instead, we simply coded occurrences of "right" on a case-by-case basis and updated the word count accordingly. This process was repeated for words like "Nazi" in order to ensure the accurate measurement of the focus on World War II vis-à-vis postwar extremism.

Step 6: Analyze. Once the data are generated they can be used for any relevant statistical purpose.

The key concepts counts are displayed in Figure 2.1.

We recommend the following first steps:

(1) Examine the relative frequency of each key concept (see Appendix Table A2.1).

(2) Test to see whether the difference in observed concepts is statistically significant. It is important to use an appropriate joint test, such as

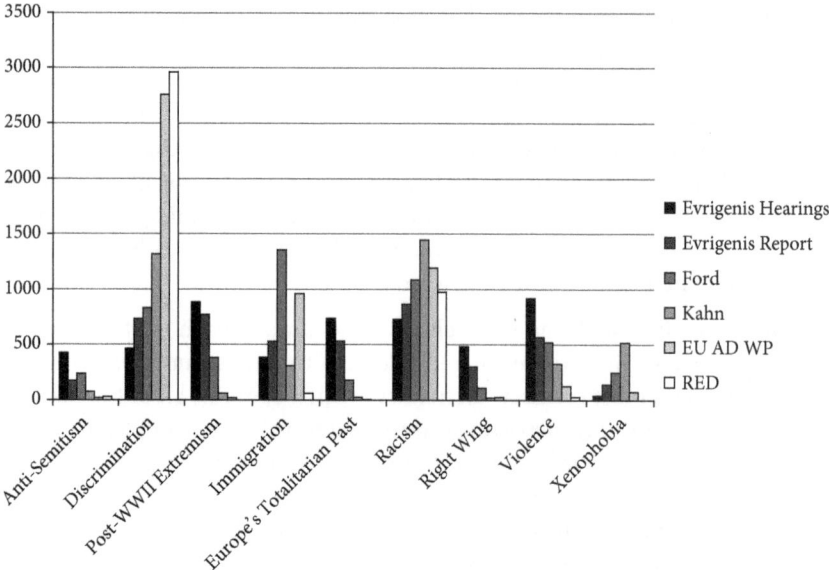

Figure 2.1 Key concept counts (occurrences per 100,000 words)

ANOVA or t-tests with an adjusted p-value when assessing more than two documents (see Appendix Table A2.2).[4]

(3) Examine the correlation matrix of key concepts.

2.5 FROM DISCOURSES TO POLICY

The documents we have analyzed indicate a clear shift away from the far right and violence, toward a focus on antidiscrimination policy from the Evrigenis Report in 1986 through the documents that led up to the passage of the RED in 2000.

The focus on racism was the only focus to remain relatively constant across all of the documents we examined.[5] In fact, the difference between the focus on race in the text of the RED was not different (in a statistically significant fashion) from that focus in any of the other documents we examined. The observed increase in emphasis on discrimination is unlikely to be due to chance. It also shows the near indistinguishability of the European Parliament Antidiscrimination Working Document and the Directive itself (they differ only on one out of nine measures), which provides evidence of the link between policy activists and entrepreneurs and the law. Table 2.4 shows that the occurrence of a focus on discrimination is negatively correlated with all

Table 2.4 Correlation matrix of key concepts

	Anti-Semitism	Discrimination	Postwar extremism	Immigration	Totalitarian past	Racism	Right wing	Violence	Xenophobia
Anti-Semitism	1	−0.82	0.87	0.12	0.87	−0.65	0.93	0.96	−0.15
Discrimination	−0.82	1	−0.83	−0.20	−0.76	0.34	−0.79	−0.92	−0.31
Postwar extremism	0.87	−0.83	1	0.04	0.98	−0.77	0.98	0.92	−0.24
Immigration	0.12	−0.20	0.04	1	−0.09	0.14	0.03	0.12	0.10
Totalitarian past	0.87	−0.76	0.98	−0.09	1	−0.80	0.99	0.92	−0.30
Racism	−0.65	0.34	−0.77	0.14	−0.80	1	−0.79	−0.57	0.77
Right-wing	0.93	−0.79	0.98	0.03	0.99	−0.79	1	0.95	−0.29
Violence	0.96	−0.92	0.92	0.12	0.92	−0.57	0.95	1	0.00
Xenophobia	−0.15	−0.31	−0.24	0.10	−0.30	0.77	−0.29	0.00	1

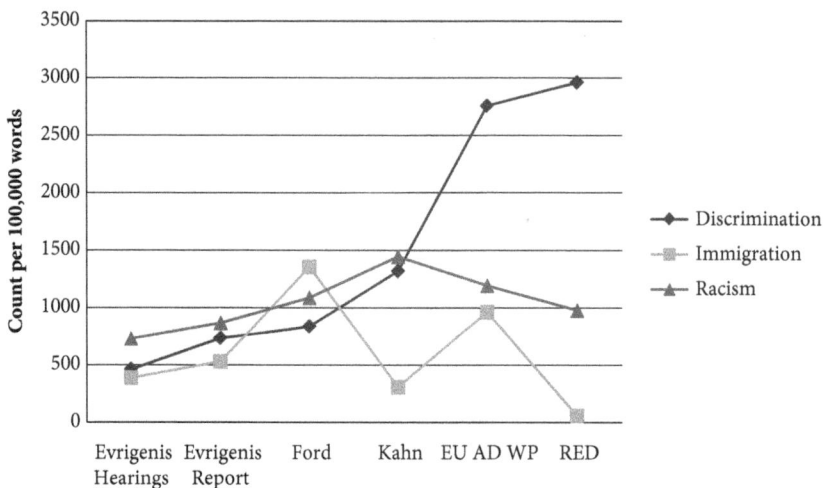

Figure 2.2 Key counts for discrimination, immigration, and racism

other concepts except racism. Thus, these tests may be taken as evidence that, at the EU level, the discourse about Europe's race problem shifted away from extremism and toward discrimination. The shift in focus to discrimination becomes clearer when comparing the documents directly on word counts for three key terms; discrimination, immigration, and racism (see Figure 2.2). This shift in discourses ultimately facilitated the passage of antidiscrimination legislation, both at the EU and the national level.

2.6 CONCLUSION

Our analysis has traced the development of ideas that ultimately led to the passage of the EU's Racial Equality Directive. Over time, key documents indicated the shift in discourses from a focus on anti-racism and the far right, to a focus on discrimination. These shifts were initiated by key players who clearly had a strategy in mind, but this analysis indicates how these strategies translated into reports and ultimately Treaty changes that would define the problem in a very different way than it was initially introduced by the European Parliament.

The data confirm that there was an initial Discourse I that was more oriented toward an anti-fascist approach that focused on racist violence and the shift to Discourse II with a focus on antidiscrimination which was initiated by the Starting Line Group in the early 1990s and dominated the documentation and the discourses by the end of the 1990s. The rest of this book will examine these developments in detail, and then follow the implementation of the Equality Directives at the national level up through 2010.

The study of institutions is about the way that rules shape outcomes. This creates a dilemma for any institutionalist approach when rules change. DI is a promising method because of the way that it focuses attention at the intersection between politics, policies, and institutions. Focusing on how extremist politics translated into party politics and discourses about hate in the 1980s and 1990s not only sheds light on the final RED policy but also helps explain why leading European politicians pushed to change the rules by expanding EU competence through the Treaty of Amsterdam.

Discursive institutionalism represents an improvement over existing institutionalist frameworks. Historical institutionalism would be well-suited to identify, for example, the European Commission's ongoing pro-integration stance, but HI is less well-suited to identify the role particular, more transient, actors, like MEP Glyn Ford, played in shaping debate. Sociological institutionalism is well-suited to identify the role that experts (such as lawyers and policy entrepreneurs) play in fashioning policies such as the RED, but, like historical institutionalism, it is ill-suited to explaining the timing of change. Rational choice institutionalism is well-suited to identify the interests that particular institutions had in transferring more or less sovereignty to the supranational level, but, on its own, RCI offers little insight into the dynamic role ideas about extremism and discrimination played in transforming those interests. DI can integrate insight from existing methodological paradigms while insisting that attention should be paid to those ideas that stitch together policy, parties, and the public.

Table A2.1 Key concept counts (occurrences per 100,000 words)

	Anti-Semitism	Discrimination	Post-WWII extremism	Immigration	Europe's totalitarian past	Racism	Right wing	Violence	Xenophobia
Evrigenis hearings	425	459	884	385	739	730	481	919	39
Evrigenis Report	172	732	770	528	530	866	299	564	142
Ford	236	834	380	1355	178	1087	109	518	248
Kahn	75	1317	58	308	23	1445	17	325	517
EU AD WP	19	2758	19	962	5	1193	24	127	75
RED	29	2961	0	58	0	978	0	29	0

Table A2.2 Tests for difference of means, by concept and document

	Evrigenis hearings	Evrigenis Report	Ford	Kahn	EU AD WP	RED
Anti-Semitism						
Evrigenis hearings		True	True	True	True	True
Evrigenis Report	< 0.001		False	True	True	False
Ford	< 0.001	0.014		True	True	True
Kahn	< 0.001	0.001	< 0.001		False	False
EU AD WP	< 0.001	< 0.001	< 0.001	0.014		False
RED	< 0.001	< 0.001	< 0.001	0.190	0.743	
Discrimination						
Evrigenis hearings		True	True	True	True	True
Evrigenis Report	< 0.001		False	True	True	True
Ford	< 0.001	0.601		True	True	True
Kahn	< 0.001	< 0.001	< 0.001		True	True
EU AD WP	< 0.001	< 0.001	< 0.001	< 0.001		False
RED	< 0.001	< 0.001	< 0.001	< 0.001	0.762	
Post-WWII extremism						
Evrigenis hearings		False	True	True	True	True
Evrigenis Report	0.029		True	True	True	True
Ford	< 0.001	< 0.001		True	True	True
Kahn	< 0.001	< 0.001	< 0.001		False	False
EU AD WP	< 0.001	< 0.001	< 0.001	0.058		False
RED	< 0.001	< 0.001	< 0.001	0.391	0.743	
Immigration						
Evrigenis hearings		False	True	False	True	True
Evrigenis Report	< 0.001		True	False	True	True
Ford	< 0.001	< 0.001		True	False	True
Kahn	0.104	< 0.001	< 0.001		True	False
EU AD WP	< 0.001	< 0.001	< 0.001	< 0.001		True
RED	< 0.001	< 0.001	< 0.001	< 0.001	< 0.001	

(*Continued*)

Table A2.2 (Continued)

	Evrigenis hearings	Evrigenis Report	Ford	Kahn	EU AD WP	RED
Europe's totalitarian past						
Evrigenis hearings		True	True	True	True	True
Evrigenis Report	< 0.001		True	True	True	True
Ford	< 0.001	< 0.001		True	True	True
Kahn	< 0.001	< 0.001	< 0.001		False	False
EU AD WP	< 0.001	< 0.001	< 0.001	0.140		False
RED	< 0.001	< 0.001	< 0.001	0.858	0.409	
Racism						
Evrigenis hearings		False	True	True	True	False
Evrigenis Report	0.009		False	True	False	False
Ford	< 0.001	< 0.001		False	False	False
Kahn	< 0.001	< 0.001	< 0.001		False	False
EU AD WP	< 0.001	< 0.001	0.206	0.032		False
RED	0.143	0.512	0.527	0.014	0.242	
Right wing						
Evrigenis hearings		True	True	True	True	True
Evrigenis Report	< 0.001		True	True	True	True
Ford	< 0.001	< 0.001		True	True	True
Kahn	< 0.001	< 0.001	< 0.001		False	False
EU AD WP	< 0.001	< 0.001	< 0.001	0.672		False
RED	< 0.001	< 0.001	< 0.001	0.709	0.865	
Violence						
Evrigenis hearings		True	True	True	True	True
Evrigenis Report	< 0.001		False	True	True	True
Ford	< 0.001	0.288		False	True	True
Kahn	< 0.001	< 0.001	< 0.001		False	True
EU AD WP	< 0.001	< 0.001	< 0.001	< 0.001		False
RED	< 0.001	< 0.001	< 0.001	< 0.001	0.009	

(*Continued*)

Table A2.2 (Continued)

	Evrigenis hearings	Evrigenis Report	Ford	Kahn	EU AD WP	RED
Xenophobia						
Evrigenis hearings		True	True	True	True	False
Evrigenis Report	< 0.001		True	True	False	False
Ford	< 0.001	< 0.001		True	True	True
Kahn	< 0.001	< 0.001	< 0.001		True	True
EU AD WP	0.069	0.009	< 0.001	< 0.001		False
RED	0.733	0.001	< 0.001	< 0.001	0.175	

NOTES

* This chapter was written with Pete Mohanty.
1. Schmidt (2008, 2011); see also Lichbach (2003); Hall and Taylor (1996); Pierson (2003).
2. For an additional example, see Armony and Armony 2009.
3. See yoshikoder.org and <http://www.abbyy.com>.
4. See, for example, Rutherford (2011).
5. See European Commission (1997); European Council (1995, 2000); European Parliament (1985).

3

The Development of Racial Antidiscrimination Policy at the National Level*

3.1 ANTIDISCRIMINATION POLICY

In this chapter, we examine national-level starting points for antidiscrimination law. The Equality Directives would ultimately have to be incorporated into existing law, but more importantly, would draw on existing legal traditions, particularly from the UK. The passage and implementation of the RED would be influenced by existing antidiscrimination policy in Europe, which provides the context for actions taken by leaders when the issue rose on the agenda at the EU level. Antidiscrimination policy was developed in the context of immigration policy, but it is also important to examine the ways in which each country approached antidiscrimination policy in terms of legal traditions and politics, particularly left party interest in these issues. Existing policy helps us to analyze the development of the RED in two main ways. First, it informs the negotiating positions of member states, and second, it shapes the process of transposing the RED. Here we provide an overview of each of our three countries' antidiscrimination policy regimes.

Policies concerning race tend to consist of two main types. The first set of policies addresses what Erik Bleich (2003: 9–13) calls "expressive racism" which includes hate speech and crimes that are racially motivated. In this category, we also place laws that prohibit the formation of racist or xenophobic groups and the dissemination of racist or xenophobic materials.[1] These policies tend to be enforced through criminal sanctions that are levied by courts. Difficulties in terms of establishing guilt have generally meant that prosecutions are few and far between. In addition, these types of policies often generate criticism for infringing the traditional civil liberties of freedom of thought, speech, and assembly. The second set of policies addresses what Bleich (2003: 9–13) calls "access racism" which includes discrimination in terms of access to employment, housing, and goods and services as well as public services and benefits. These policies were developed at the state and provincial levels in North America as early as the 1940s, but their adoption accelerated in the 1960s and 1970s. They are generally enforced through administrative procedures that seek conciliation or through civil litigation that is pursued by an aggrieved individual or by a government agency acting on an individual's behalf. Although proposals for both types of policies have been made at the EU level, the RED addresses only the latter of the two.

We show that Britain began developing "race relations" policies as ethnic minority immigration became a concern in the 1960s. By contrast, both France and Germany had constitutional commitments to equality and non-discrimination on grounds of race, among other grounds, but neither country followed the British model. France deliberately rejected an approach that focused policy on specific groups, while Germany refused to accept that immigrants had become settlers.

Mark Bell argues that, prior to the transposition of the EU Directives discussed above, the members of EU-15 could be broadly classified into three sets: "Equality Law Regimes," "Anti-Discrimination Law Regimes," and states without specific anti-discrimination legislation (see Table 3.1). The main difference between the Equality Law Regimes and Anti-Discrimination Law Regimes (the U.S. would be classified as the latter) is that lawmakers in Equality Law Regimes have come to view the proscription of discrimination—the "largely negative obligation" to abstain from particular practices with respect to, say, hiring—as inadequate and have taken a more proactive stance. Bell writes that:

> States with *equality* laws have recognized the limits of an anti-discrimination strategy dependent on individual litigants and have responded principally in two directions. First, institutional provision has been made to support individual litigants, with a view to rendering more effective and accessible the right to non-discrimination. Second, measures have been adopted which break the link with the individual plaintiff, thereby focusing on collective mechanisms...This frequently manifests itself in the adoption of positive action. Such measures include making public procurement contracts conditional on firms meeting equality requirements...monitoring the workplace...and targeting advertisements at groups currently underrepresented in the workforce. (Bell 2002: 148)

Bell adds that the best existing example of such positive action, at the time, was to be found in the campaign against religious discrimination in Northern Ireland. Bell suggests that it is useful to further subdivide Equality Law Regimes and Anti-Discrimination Law Regimes into "comprehensive" and "mixed level" regimes, depending on whether the member state protects all or only some of the classes that would come to be protected by the EU Equality Directives.

Table 3.1 Non-discrimination law regimes in the EU-15 prior to the Equality
Directives

Equality law regimes		Antidiscrimination law regimes		States without specific antidiscrimination legislation
Comprehensive	Mixed-level	Comprehensive	Mixed-level	
Netherlands, Ireland, and Sweden	Britain, Belgium, and Italy	Denmark, France, Luxembourg, Finland, and Spain	Portugal and Germany	Austria and Greece

Source: Adapted from Bell (2002: 145ff.).

3.2 INTERNATIONAL DEVELOPMENTS

The word "discrimination" does not appear in the UN Charter or in the
Universal Declaration of Human Rights (UDHR), but it quickly became a
major subject of interest within United Nations (UN) bodies. In 1949, the UN
Secretary-General issued a memorandum on "The Main Types and Causes of
Discrimination," explaining a concept that was still unfamiliar to most readers.
In the years that followed, numerous seminars were convened on the problems
of race and racial discrimination.[2]

His memorandum identified three types of measures that could be employed
to counter discrimination: (1) direct legal action; (2) administrative measures
put into effect by public agencies; and, (3) educational action (1949: 5, para.
17). It also recognized a suggestion offered by Dr. Gunnar Myrdal that independent legal aid services manned by highly qualified professional lawyers
be established to assist complainants in the enforcement of their legal rights
(1949: 48–49, para. 155).

In particular, attention focused primarily on racial difference. Subsequent
geopolitical circumstances, namely the Cold War and decolonization, maintained that attention on race, particularly white oppression of non-whites. At
about the same time, efforts to use the UN as a tool against racism and racial
discrimination intensified. In 1965, the United Nations General Assembly
(UNGA) submitted the International Covenant on the Elimination of All
Forms of Racial Discrimination (ICERD) to member states for ratification.
The UNGA declared 1971 the International Year against Racism and designated 1973 as the beginning of a Decade for Action to Combat Racism
and Racial Discrimination.[3] "At the national level, the vast majority agreed
to provide assistance to victims of racial discrimination, to abrogate any
policies or regulations of their own that had the effect of creating or per-
petuating racial hatred, to nullify any immigration laws based upon race, to
provide legal protection for basic human rights, and to deny any political

Table 3.2 Ratification of International Convention on the Elimination of All Forms of Racial Discrimination (ICERD)

EU member states	Ratification of ICERD	Domestic legislation
Germany	1969	2006
United Kingdom	1969	1965
France	1971	1972
Netherlands	1972	1981
Belgium	1975	1986

Note: The date used here is the date that the Convention entered into force.

or diplomatic support to governments that practice racial discrimination" (Lauren 1988: 235).

EU member states were previously confronted with international pressure to adopt antidiscrimination laws, and several countries did ratify some conventions. In 1965, the UN adopted the ICERD. However, as Table 3.2 indicates, ratification did not necessarily lead to domestic legislation, at least not immediately.

International agreements appear to have influenced some countries to adopt antidiscrimination laws, but as we will see below in the case studies of Britain, France, and Germany, some were more comprehensive than others.

3.3 ANTIDISCRIMINATION POLICY IN BRITAIN, FRANCE, AND GERMANY

As discussed in the introduction, Britain, France, and Germany are three key players both in terms of the development of the European Union, and in terms of the flow of immigrants into Europe. These case studies provide a range of the types of developments related to antidiscrimination policy in Europe and also demonstrate the types of policy that would ultimately impact the adoption of the Equality Directives at the EU level.

3.3.1 Britain and Antidiscrimination Law

Of the three cases considered in this book, Britain has the most developed race policy history, and by 2000, it had the highest degree of policy fit with the RED in terms of both general policy and technical legal requirements.

Table 3.3 British race relations laws

1965	Race Relations Act—creates a criminal offense related to incitement of racial hatred and outlaws discrimination in access to premises.
1968	Race Relations Act—outlaws discrimination more thoroughly, in employment and housing and services.
1976	Race Relations Act—establishes the Commission for Racial Equality (CRE). Wide in scope: employment, education, housing, provision of goods, services.
2000	Race Relations Act—1976 Act amended to include all functions of public authorities.

Antidiscrimination law and immigration restrictions developed in tandem in Britain, as the political elite sought to reduce the number of new immigrants and to devise ways of integrating existing immigrants and especially their children, the so-called "second generation," into British society. The Commonwealth Immigrants Act of 1962, the Commonwealth Immigrants Act of 1968, the Immigration Appeals Act of 1969, and the Immigration Act of 1971 were followed by new race relations legislation in 1965, 1968, and 1976 (see Table 3.3). British policy was greatly influenced by policy developments in North America. As Andrew Geddes and Virginie Guiraudon (2004: 338) observe, in the 1960s, "ideas about 'race,' 'racial difference,' 'racial equality' and 'ethnic minorities' became key policy referents in the UK."

After several proposals for racial antidiscrimination legislation by individual Members of Parliament failed in the 1950s, the Labour government adopted Britain's first racial antidiscrimination law in 1965. The Race Relations Act of 1965 made it illegal to discriminate in hotels, public houses, restaurants, theatres, public transport, and any place maintained by a public authority. The Bill had originally proposed making discrimination a criminal offense punishable by fines of up to £100, but the idea of criminal sanctions generated considerable opposition. As a result, the criminal sanctions were replaced with a mechanism for conciliation between the aggrieved and offending parties. Where conciliation failed, local committees could report to a Race Relations Board that could then refer the case to the Attorney General, who possessed the authority to go to court and obtain an injunction against the offending party. As Zig Layton-Henry (1984: 130) observes, this act "was intended to have a declaratory effect." By design, it sought "to encourage people to do what was right by conciliation" rather than "suppress acts of racial discrimination by legal sanctions."

Three years later, the Race Relations Act was replaced with a new law that expanded the scope of the law's application and reformed the enforcement mechanisms. The Race Relations Act of 1968 added employment, housing, and the provision of commercial and other services to the list of areas in which discrimination was prohibited. In addition, it authorized the Race Relations

Board to investigate complaints of discriminatory behavior, institute conciliation procedures, and, as a last resort, pursue legal proceedings in order to
secure compliance with the new law. Although the Act prohibited the Crown
from discriminating, it exempted the Crown from any proceedings in the
courts. In subsequent years, it became clear that the problem of discrimination continued and the legislation was again revised in 1976.

The Race Relations Act of 1976 expanded the scope and enforcement of
antidiscrimination policy.[4] It broadened the scope of the law to prohibit discrimination in training and related matters and in education. Although it did
not do so in express terms, the Act also distinguished between *direct* and *indirect* discrimination. In terms of enforcement, the Act abandoned the earlier
system of administrative conciliation and provided individuals with a right to
initiate civil proceedings directly in court.[5] It also established the Commission
for Racial Equality, a non-departmental public body that was empowered to
conduct formal investigations as well as provide legal assistance to individual
complainants. In addition, other organizations, such as trade unions and professional associations, were also authorized to support an individual's complaint of discrimination in court. Under the 1976 Act, the burden of proof lay
with the complainant, although the Act included a procedure through which
an individual could seek to obtain information from the alleged discrimina-
tor prior to initiating litigation. The Race Relations Act of 1976 applied to acts
performed by the Crown in the same way as it applied to acts performed by a
private person. In *Amin* v. *Entry Clearance Officer, Bombay* [1983] 1A C 818,
the House of Lords held that the Act did not apply to governmental and regulatory activities, such as immigration control, administration of the prison system, and the law enforcement activities of the police, although it did apply to
the provision of services. Although the CRE had advocated legislative reform
that would change this, the government did not do so until 2000.

A major turn in antidiscrimination law began in April 1993 with the murder
of a young, black, A-level student, Stephen Lawrence, in southeast London. The
events surrounding the subsequent investigation have been detailed in many
studies (e.g., Bleich 2003; BBC 1999).[6] When New Labour came to power in
1997, there was a clear shift in emphasis to address racial injustice. With the
failure to convict the main suspects in the case, due to the bungled police
investigation, the new government commissioned the McPherson Report,
published in February 1999. The report highlighted the impact of "institutional racism" in the ethnic minority community of Britain and made many
policy recommendations that would strengthen the 1976 Race Relations Act.

A direct result of the McPherson Report was the 2000 Race Relations
(Amendment) Act that extended coverage of the 1976 Act to the police and
other public officials previously exempt from the laws against discrimination.
It holds chief officers liable for acts of racism by policemen and women under
their supervision, creating a strong incentive for them to enact internal policies

that root out racism. The Act also places a "general duty" on public authorities as diverse as the army, governing bodies of schools, and sewage authorities to eliminate discrimination and to promote equality of opportunity and positive relations between individuals of different racial groups (Small and Solomos 2006). Small and Solomos point out that there was "disappointment that the Act did not take up all of the recommendations made by the commission for Racial Equality...Perhaps the most telling section of the Act was Section 19, which excluded immigration and asylum and refuge from the remit of the Act" (Small and Solomos 2006: 246). This exclusion was a precursor to a major shift in focus during Labour's second term in office.

In addition to the foregoing laws that addressed access racism, Britain also adopted several laws that addressed expressive and physical racism.[7] For example, even before the publication of the McPherson Report, the New Labour government enacted the Crime and Disorder Act 1998. This measure enables prosecutors and courts to impose stiffer penalties for crimes motivated by racial animus. The law explicitly embeds crimes of physical racism into the country's institutional repertoire.

3.3.2 France

As with Germany, French constitutional law expresses a firm commitment to equality. Article 1 of the French Constitution of October 4, 1958 provides that "France ensures the equality before the law of all citizens, without distinction of origin, race or religion." In addition, the preamble provides that "...the people of France proclaim anew that each human being, without distinction of race, religion or belief, possesses sacred inalienable rights," and it reaffirms the rights and freedoms set forth in the Declaration of Rights of 1789.[8]

In stark contrast to Britain, France has historically rejected the very concept of "race." Thus, France rejected the idea of recognizing and classifying individuals in terms of race and ethnicity, preferring instead the concept of a French people comprising French citizens. This view is reflected in its constitutional law. Article 1 of the 1958 Constitution, which provides for "equality before the law of all citizens without distinction of origin, race, or religion," has been interpreted to prohibit the drawing of distinctions. As a result, the French state does not collect data on racial or ethnic groups (Radcliffe 2001). In fact, a 1978 law on data storage prohibited the maintenance of data on racial and ethnic origins without the individual's express consent or formal permission by a national commission (Geddes and Guiraudon 2004: 339).[9] This view shaped French policy in important ways.

When it comes to dealing with acts of discrimination, France relies upon a criminal law approach. It has had anti-racist legislation on its books since 1972, when it enacted a law that criminalized racial discrimination and hate

Table 3.4 Antidiscrimination legislation in France, 1972–1994

Law 72-546—July 1, 1972—racial discrimination made illegal. The law introduces Article 416 into the Penal Code, penalizing certain conduct, such as refusal or conditional offer of goods, services, employment (and dismissal).

Law 75-625—July 11, 1975—combating discrimination no longer restricted to race, adding sex and family situation.

Law 77-574—June 7, 1977—supplements the list from 1972, adding interference in the exercise of economic activity on the basis of race.

Law 85-772—July 25, 1985—makes discrimination based on customs illegal.

Law 89-18—January 13, 1989 and Law 90-602 of July 12, 1990 add disability and state of health to the list of grounds of discrimination.

Law of July 22, 1992 (coming into force on March 1, 1994) reforms the Penal Code and simplifies the definition of offenses. It also adds discrimination on the grounds of political opinion and union activity to the list of punishable discriminations. It increases the established penalties.

New Penal Code of 1994 establishes Articles 225-1 and 225-2. 225-1 establishes a definition of discrimination and 225-2 specifies cases in which it is punishable and what penalties are to be imposed. Also, Article 432-7 prohibits discrimination by representatives of public authorities.

speech. It underwent further developments and reform as noted in Table 3.4. This early law recognized an enforcement role for civil organizations. It promoted the role of *parties civiles* (civil parties) in the fight against racism.

According to Bell (1998: 31), during the 1980s, between 80 and 90 discrimination cases were pursued annually, rising to 101 in 1991, but the number of employment cases is between three and four annually. These numbers contrast with the British case, where in 1996, 90 percent of the cases taken to court were employment related. Convictions were very rare in the French case (Costa-Lascoux 1994). Between 1975 and 1984, approximately 160 cases were reported to the Justice Ministry, and from 1984 to 1988, the annual number of convictions for race-related offense fluctuated between 95 and 66 (Costa-Lascoux 1994). Lieberman found that annual convictions between 1993 and 1997 ranged between 61 and 95, and 90 percent of those convictions involved racist expression rather than racial discrimination (Lieberman 2005: 155). Indeed, during those years, only seven of 380 convictions were for employment discrimination.

Rejection of "race" as a concept and, in turn, the collection of data on racial or ethnic groups affected the ability to determine the extent of discrimination, particularly in employment in France. However, in February 1990, two published decrees authorized the *Services de Renseignments* to collect and archive "racial origins." This development inspired the creation of an association whose goal was to keep the word "race" out of the

Constitution. Debates ranged from senators and historians to philosophers, sociologists, and geneticists who were concerned that these decrees presented a risk of judicial consecration and legitimization of the notion of race (Calvés 2002).

While it has taken many shapes, Calvés noted that ten years later the same question was still being asked. She argues that public policy does not aim to combat racism, but discrimination. Also, the discussion is not one of "race" but of "ethnicity." There appear to be two reasons for this. The first concerns the integration of immigrants—to avoid the continued distinction (interpreted as a negative) for second- and third-generation immigrants. This would create the categories of French-by-attribution and the French-by-acquisition. Questions along these lines were raised in the 1986 Code of Nationality, and gave rise to the 1990 *Haut Conseil à l'Integration* (which quickly took a statistical focus). In that same year the *Commission Nationale Consultative des Droits de l'Homme* released a report that was later published by the *Institut National d'Etudes Démographiques* (INED and INSEE 1992). The distinction between "foreigner" and "French" was abandoned in the interest of "science" (and evidently politics). New administrations were created, and the missions of others revised, to "promote integration" and "combat racism." Examples include: *Agence pour le développement des relations interculterelles, Groupe d'etude et de lutte contre les discriminations*, and the FAS, which became *Fonds d'action et de soutien pour l'integration et la lutte contre les discriminations* in February 2002.[10] What most of these had in common was their focus on observing, or "ethnic monitoring." This focus, combined with the French taboo on recognizing race, caused a shift in focus from anti-racism to an emphasis on the notions of "rights" and politics. This was a setback in the struggle against racism and necessitated the use of a new hypocritical code: ghetto youth, immigrant French, Black, etc., to describe a growing reality of discrimination.[11]

In terms of enforcing French laws against racism, French law permits unions and associations to act as civil claimants.[12] With regard to the latter, they must have been legally established for five years at the time of the incident.[13] France lacked a body that was expressly charged with receiving complaints of discrimination and pressing for prosecutions, but the Commission on Access to Citizenship was expressly authorized to inform legal authorities about incidents of discrimination for investigation or prosecution.

The Criminal Code (Art. 225-1) defines discrimination in a general way: "Any discrimination defined as the refusal to provide goods or services, refusal to employ an individual, unfair sanctions or dismissal, or hindering normal economic activity on the grounds of somebody's 'race,' religion or origins constitutes a criminal offense" (Schnapper et al. 2003: 27). Although it does not contain definitions of direct and indirect discrimination, as the RED requires, its language is sufficiently broad to encompass both types of discrimination through judicial interpretation. The New Penal Code, which entered into force in 1994, makes it illegal for public authorities to discriminate (Art. 432-7). However, as Sophie Recht (2002) observes, examples of prosecutions beyond labor and press law were rare.

In their article on racial discrimination[14] Dhume and Noel (1999) argue that minority youth have become stigmatized, and while they generally experience a strong cultural integration, they experience weak social and professional integration. On October 21, 1998 the *Ministre de l'Emploi et de la Solidarité* (Minister of Employment and Solidarity) recommended the creation of a committee against discrimination in order to address these types of issues. The decision was influenced by the recommendations of the *Commission Nationale Consultative des Droits de l'Homme*.[15] The work of this commission and others suggests that racial discrimination is widespread, but its political, cultural, and economic and financial effects are little explored. This is largely because of the informality of prejudicial practices, which often occur in passing conversation (Dhume and Noel 1999).

In 1999 the GELD (*Groupe d'Etude et de Lutte contre les Discriminations*)[16] set out to analyze discrimination (real or imagined), to explain the mechanisms at work, and to identify methods to combat it. Similarly, Calvés finds that there was a legislative turnaround between 1997 and 2000. For example a 2000 Directive sought to identify "apparently neutral" categories, when a person might be susceptible to disadvantage because of race or ethnicity relative to others. However, this still left room for decisions to be made based on stereotype or prejudice (Calvés 2002).

Rather than try to define discrimination through categories, another approach was taken, allowing people to report discrimination. In May 2000, the phone-in hotline "114" was established which is a free, universal hotline on which to report discrimination based on origin. Also, from July 1998 to May 2000 a series of communiqués requested the vigilance of public servants and the employees of local and national governments in the fight against discrimination based on sex or race. Finally, a May 2, 2000 Directive was put forward, set to cultivate role models for youth of color who displayed academic, athletic, professional, and social success (Calvés 2002).

Virginie Guiraudon (2004) examines developments in antidiscrimination policy between 1997 and 2000, particularly in France. She focuses on the actions of specific leaders, such as Alain Juppé, the leader of the conservative RPR (Rally for the Republic) who realized that there was a possibility of attracting immigrant voters. During this time, the right began to consider making antidiscrimination policy a priority.

In October 1999, the former Gaullist Prime Minister Alain Juppé declared in a *Le Monde* interview that given that in some areas, 50 percent of immigrant youth was unemployed and felt discriminated against in the job market, an antidiscrimination policy would show them that they had the same rights and preserve "national cohesion." In his view, given that "the economic context was more favorable," this policy could generate support. The RPR leader had realized that as populations of migrant origin became more diversified socially, they were likely to be more politically diverse as well and not only left-leaning as when they were comprised of factory workers (Geddes and Giraudon 2002: 26). Juppé's position indicated that it was not only left leaders who would consider a change in antidiscrimination policy, and also recognized the potential for electoral competition over the issue.

It is clear that by 2000, France had adjusted some technical aspects of its policy in ways that would fit with the RED, but at a general policy level there was still some resistance to accepting the idea of race. Although France had moved slightly closer in the years immediately preceding the RED's adoption, it still evidenced a low degree of fit. However, France was clearly in a position that was more open to antidiscrimination policy than Germany, as we will see below.

3.3.3 Germany

Someone familiar with postwar constitutional jurisprudence in Germany might be surprised to discover the amount of practical difficulty that Germany has had transposing the RED. Commentators on affirmative action in the United States have noted how the free speech provisions of the First Amendment have been an obstacle to stronger readings of the equal protection provision of the Fourteenth Amendment (Matsuda and Lawrence 1993). However, this is not the case in Germany, where the law allows for "banning of racist groups as well as punishment of incitement to racial hatred" (Bleich 2003: 201). Furthermore, in Germany, writes Catherine Dupré, "although fundamental rights are given priority in the German Basic Law, they are by no means absolute" (2003: 123). This is because the German Constitutional Court interprets the Basic Law provision protecting the right each has to the "free development of his personality" to mean that individuals have rights but, also, that individuals must be considered to be part of a community with responsibilities toward others (Glendon 1991: 61; Dupré 2003: 123). Thus, though there are more obstacles to antidiscrimination policy in Germany than there are in the (parliamentary) United Kingdom, there are far fewer constitutional obstacles to antidiscrimination policy in Germany than there are in the United States. On the other hand, "the term race is absent from German structures, as it remains taboo in light of the Nazi experience" (Bleich 2003: 201). So what was the state of antidiscrimination law in Germany at the time of RED transposition?

Prior to its transposition of the RED in 2006, Germany did not have specific legislation that prohibited racial or ethnic discrimination in the private and public spheres. Instead, it had an assortment of laws that addressed issues pertaining to racial and ethnic discrimination in various areas of life. In important ways, these laws reflected German commitments to the public–private divide. Very few cases were pursued under the assemblage of laws. First, the application of these laws was limited in scope. Second, they did not provide adequate remedies. German law offers protection against racial discrimination within the public sphere, but within the private sphere, it offers protections against discrimination on grounds of gender, but not race. Article 3.1 of the German Constitution (known as the Basic Law, or *Grundgesetz*) contains a general guarantee of equal treatment, and Article 3.3 prohibits discrimination by reasons of sex, parentage, race, language, homeland and origin, faith, religious or political opinions, or disabilities.[17] These constitutional provisions apply across the public realm, including healthcare, education, police law, and social law. Article 3 operates both *directly* and *indirectly* upon the state. It applies directly *only* to actions taken by the state. Thus, it generally guarantees that statutes will not be applied in a discriminatory fashion.[18] This applies to actions taken by the government but not to private actors carrying out the provision of public services. Indirectly, Article 3 may influence judicial interpretation of civil law in cases in which an individual complains of discrimination that was committed by a private actor (Won-Pil Suh and Bales 2006: 292), but importantly, it does not apply to actions taken by citizens in the private sphere. With regard to the public sector, the Federal Civil Services Code (*Bundesbeamtengesetz*) prohibits "differentiation" on the basis of religion and origin, among other grounds. Individuals may invoke Article 3 before the administrative courts or the Federal Constitutional Court.[19]

The German Constitutional Court (*Bundesverfassungsgericht*) has had several occasions to interpret Article 3 in terms of sex discrimination. It has made two innovative decisions. First, it has recognized that the constitutional provision encompasses both direct *and* indirect discrimination. Second, the general equality clause has been strengthened. Traditionally, it was interpreted as prohibiting arbitrary decisions, but the Court has developed a strict test of proportionality. The burden of justifying discrimination has been increased. Nevertheless, there are exceptions to the principle of equal treatment. Religious communities, for example, can make affiliation and comportment with religious standards of behavior a precondition for employment. Further, exceptions may be made when there are legitimate grounds for unequal treatment and the differentiation is proportionate.

Germany lacks a comprehensive antidiscrimination policy regime that applies to private actors and institutions. Instead, there exists an assemblage of laws that are spread across a variety of different statutes. In the private law realm, the principle of equality competes with another constitutional value, the right to individual and contractual freedom as guaranteed by Article 2.1 (Won-Pil Suh and Bales 2006). In order to comply with EU Directives concerning gender discrimination, reforms have been made. Germany lacked comprehensive protection against discrimination in the workplace and in the context of other legal contracts, although it did prohibit gender discrimination (DGB §§ 611a, arbeitsrecht.de, 2006). German law did not expressly provide protection from discrimination by private entities, and it did not regulate discrimination (aside from gender discrimination) in the contractual relationship between employer and employee (Won-Pil Suh and Bales 2006: 291–92).

Section 75 of the Employment Constitution Act (December 23, 1988) (*B etriebsverfassungsgesetz BetrVG*) obligated employers and works councils to ensure that all employees are treated "according to the principles of justice and equity, and in particular that there is no discriminatory treatment of persons on grounds of their extraction, religion, nationality, origin, or political or trade union activity or attitude, or on grounds of sex." This Act, however, only applied "to private sector companies in which a works council has to be formed, i.e., that have at least five permanent employees" (Mahlmann 2002: 11). It does not apply to the recruitment stage of the employment process. Because of constitutional commitments, this Act does not apply to enterprises and organizations that are "directly and predominantly of a political, coalitional, confessional, charitable, educational, academic or artistic nature or that serve to report information or express an opinion, in as much as this would conflict with the nature of the said enterprise or organization" (Mahlmann 2002: 11). Employees who allege discrimination are required to lodge a complaint with the employer, who is obligated to investigate the complaint. If the complaint is found to be justified, the employer is further obligated to remedy the situation. In cases not covered by the Works Constitution Act, employees who (believe that they) have been discriminated against at their workplace can only invoke the employer's general obligation to take care of its employees.

German law did not contain definitions of direct or indirect discrimination based on racial or ethnic origin. Nor does it contain a definition of racial harassment. Some acts that are intended to intimidate or create a hostile environment may constitute libel or slander and may therefore be pursued under section 185 of the criminal code (STGB). German law does not prohibit instructions to discriminate. However, as Mahlmann (2002: 15) notes, "the instruction to discriminate could be regarded as the instigation to commit libel or slander" under section 26, 185 STGB. If a public official issues such instructions, then the resultant administrative act would breach Article 3 of the Basic Law and be illegal. In addition, the principle of equal rights in German labor law prohibited discrimination against nationals of other EU member states (Civil Code § 611a, 612(3)).

In contrast to the RED, German law stated that NGOs are not entitled to initiate legal proceedings on behalf of aggrieved individuals. Additionally, there are no representative actions. There is "very little case law—apart from criminal proceedings concerning hate crimes—that deal with discrimination on the basis of race and ethnic origin" (Malhman 2003: 5). Germany lacked an independent body charged with promoting equality for racial and ethnic minorities, although at both the federal and state levels there are Commissioners for Foreigners' Affairs (*Die Beauftragte für Ausländerfragen*). These bodies, however, are not so charged, although they review policy concerning migrants and make recommendations. The federal commissioner is located in the Ministry of Labor and Social Affairs. In 1996, these bodies organized the publication of a *Legal Guide on the Protection against Discrimination* (see Nickel 1996). The Commissioner for Foreigners is charged with aiding the "integration" of migrants to Germany, to help the government develop its "integration" policy, as well as to combat discrimination. In recent years, governments have established several programs for the coordination of local activities, including the Forum against Racism (est. 1998), the Alliance for Democracy and Tolerance against Extremism and Violence (est. 2000), and the German Institute for Human Rights (est. 2001).

Religious institutions, which include hospitals as well as churches, maintain a right to refuse employment to persons holding different religious beliefs. As a strong religious center, Bavaria has proven a contested area. Due to its historical experience with Nazism, Germany today has laws that limit the formation and operation of radical right political parties. Various studies of societal attitudes and behavior toward non-whites demonstrate that despite the inability to mobilize politically, there are strong pockets of racist views within society. There have been many examples of attacks on people of immigrant origin, including skinhead attacks in Berlin and the eastern states after reunification.

Although Germany has limited laws on discrimination, they differ fundamentally from those required by the RED. As Bleich has noted, "Germany has laws that permit the banning of racist groups as well as punishment of incitement to racial hatred" (Bleich 2003: 201), and there is little focus on issues such as discrimination in employment. Despite the existence of these laws, it is difficult for minorities to take advantage of them, both because of the lack of clear prohibitions, and the fact that most minorities are not citizens.

3.4 CONCLUSION

The greatest legacy of the postcolonial and labor migrations in Britain, France, and Germany is a significant foreign and immigrant-origin population. It is of great import, and yet is often overlooked, that one of the motivations for immigration reform in Europe has been the perceived inability of "foreign" populations to assimilate or of immigrants to integrate into receiving societies. Despite considerably divergent starting points, France, Britain, and Germany (as well as the other Western and Southern European countries) have all been struggling with the task of integrating, socially and economically, their immigrant and foreign-born descendant populations.

This set of challenges is quite troubling when we take into consideration that "discrimination" in Europe is almost synonymous with the debates over the "immigrant problem." Unlike the United States, where "race" has never ceased to be the focal point of social division and the most prevalent form of discrimination, Europe has "evolved" a much more "sophisticated" form of discrimination in order to circumvent norms that have been advanced since the fall of the Nazi regime. Therefore, American color-based discrimination is seen as particularly abhorrent to Western Europeans with governments in France and Germany going so far as to forbid any form of government-sponsored statistics collection on the basis of race. Only Britain had an outwardly racist immigration policy, although even there it was couched in terms of ancestry.

Antidiscrimination policy reflected concerns about the type of immigrants coming into a country, and whether or not there was a real recognition of immigrants as settlers. The three cases reflect a range of policies from Britain's race-conscious "race relations" legislation, to France's criminalization of discrimination, and Germany's lack of recognition of the issue. Based on this context, one would expect that France and Germany might be the least likely candidates to support legislation like the RED. However, events that we will describe in the next chapter pushed both countries to become supporters of the Directive. This would be a clear break in policy for both countries, at a time when controlling immigration was a major concern.

NOTES

* This chapter was written with Rhonda Evans Case.
1. There is a striking contrast between the United States and Europe on this matter, because U.S. First Amendment jurisprudence prohibits censoring speech on the basis of its content (see *R. A. V. v. St. Paul* [1992]).
2. For example, see one on the question of elimination of all forms of racial discrimination held in New Delhi, India from August 27 to September 9, 1968; one "On Measures to be Taken on the National Level for the Implementation of UN Instruments Aimed at Combating and Eliminating Racial Discrimination and for the Promotion of Harmonious Race Relations: Symposium on the Evils of Racial Discrimination" held in Yaounde, Federal Republic of Cameroon from June 16–29, 1971.
3. 2010 marked the end of the third such official decade.
4. This Act applies to Great Britain, but not to Northern Ireland.
5. The court from which an individual could seek relief depended upon the type of discrimination claim and the jurisdiction in which the discriminatory act occurred. In cases involving discrimination in employment, individuals could

go to industrial tribunals. In all other types of cases, individuals in England and Wales could go to a county court, whereas individuals in Scotland could go to a sheriff's court.

6. <http://news.bbc.co.uk/1/hi/special_report/1999/02/99/stephen_lawrence/285357.stm> accessed January 31, 2008.

7. Physical racism refers to physical attacks against persons or property motivated by racial hatred (Bleich 2003).

8. This language appears in the Preamble of the Constitution of October 27, 1946, which also serves as the Preamble for the Constitution of 1958. Based upon these provisions, the Constitutional Council has issued a number of decisions against state actions that discriminate against individuals, particularly on grounds of nationality (see Recht 2002: 11–12).

9. Article 226-19 of the Penal Code.

10. Translations: Agency for the Development of Intercultural Relations; Group for the Study of and Fight against Discrimination; Fund for Action and Support of Integration and the Fight against Discrimination.

11. Paraphrasing Calves (2002).

12. Articles L 411-11 and R 516-5 of the Labor Code and 142-20 of the Social Security Code.

13. Articles 2-1 to 2-14 of the Code of Criminal Procedure; Article 48 of the Law of July 29, 1881.

14. Translations from the French by Givens.

15. National Consultative Commission on Human Rights.

16. Group to Study and Combat Discrimination.

17. The constitutions of some of the *Länder* contain similar provisions.

18. Unless material reasons exist to justify differential treatment.

19. Constitutional and administrative complaints must be filed within 30 days of the grievance.

4

The Road to Amsterdam, Paved with Whose Intentions?*

I do not believe that we can credibly claim to support the concept of a Citizens' Europe which, for example, sets welfare standards for farm animals but remains utterly silent on the subject of racism.

Pádraig Flynn, Commissioner for Social Affairs (1995)[1]

4.1 THE PUZZLE

The previous chapter laid a foundation for understanding the political development of antidiscrimination policy at the national level and the positions that EU member states Britain, France, and Germany might take on the issue. This chapter analyzes developments at the supranational level. In 1997, 13 years after the European Parliament first placed the issue of racism on the European agenda, national governments unanimously agreed to add Article 13 to the Treaty of Amsterdam, thereby assigning the EU explicit authority to act with regard to discrimination on a number of grounds, including race and ethnic origin, and taking an important step in the effort to construct a "Citizens' Europe" (Barnard 1997: 280). They adopted the Racial Equality Directive three years later. The RED required member states to adopt within three years a specific set of national laws that prohibit discrimination on grounds of racial or ethnic origin in a wide array of public and private areas of life. Racial antidiscrimination policy was thereby unequivocally Europeanized.

In this chapter, through process tracing, we examine the development of discourses and the role and preferences of individuals in moving forward an agenda on anti-racism that ultimately led to a focus on antidiscrimination policy. We show in this chapter the role of members' left parties and advocacy groups in moving the agenda forward up until the member states unanimously approved both Article 13 and the RED. What we expect to see is the dominance of an anti-racist discourse initially, with a shift to a new discourse more focused on antidiscrimination after the Starting Line Group becomes a key player along with the European Commission in the development of policy.

4.2 KEY DEVELOPMENTS

In this chapter, we track two key developments. The first is that it was specific individuals who used the institutional structure to move forward an agenda based on a topic where it was not clear that European institutions had competency. This conclusion rests upon three critical observations that are presented through a historical narrative. First, supranational institutions, as opposed to member states, placed and maintained the problems of racism and racial discrimination on the European agenda. Secondly, and by, contrast, when national governments responded, they consistently defined the problem almost exclusively in terms of racist speech and violence, xenophobia, and the proliferation of organizations that advocate racist ideas and behavior. Until the mid-1990s, they generally refused to define the problem in terms of discrimination. Third, until the 1996–1997 Intergovernmental Conference (ICG), member states resisted calls for European policy action on the issue, either via a legislative measure pursuant to existing Treaty provisions or through an amendment to the Treaty.

The second key development is the rise of an organization made up of NGOs and activists that would push forward the agenda on antidiscrimination policy. Although the European Parliament consistently used its agenda-setting functions to define racism and discrimination as important problems that merited a supranational policy response, Parliament lacked the capacity to compel action by the Council. The Commission, too, performed a key agenda-setting function. However, it refrained from using its additional power of legislative initiative until after the TEU had been amended through a demonstration of unanimous member state support. Moreover, it did not expressly advocate for a Treaty amendment until 1994. By the mid-1990s, a loose network of transnational human rights activists and legal experts known as the Starting Line Group had joined the EP and the Commission in lobbying member states to take European action against racism and discrimination. Its initial efforts focused on securing a Directive, but when these failed, the SLG changed tactics in 1993 and pursued a Treaty amendment instead.

In analyzing these developments, it is important to take into account the complexity and interactive effects on policy processes. According to Paul Pierson (1996: 131–32), four factors are likely to create "significant divergences between the institutional and policy preferences of member states and the actual functioning of institutions and policies." These include the autonomous actions of EU actors, the restricted time horizons of decision-makers, the large potential for unintended consequences, and the likelihood of changes in the preferences of national governments over time.

Our analysis also confirms that the radical right's resurgence played an important role in the Europeanization of racial antidiscrimination policy, but not exactly in the way that liberal intergovernmentalists would predict. The need to respond to the success of the radical right moved member states to act in ways that they may not have in a different context. We begin by examining the way in which the problem of racism was defined, with the rise of the radical right as the backdrop.

4.3 THE POLITICS OF PROBLEM DEFINITION

In the 1980s and early 1990s, racist acts of violence and the stunning success of radical right political parties across Europe catapulted the issues of immigration, xenophobia, fascism, and racism to the forefront. The EP and the Commission placed these issues squarely on the supranational agenda. European political elites grappled with three main policy questions, to which EU institutions, transnational human rights activists, and member states provided very different answers. First, what exactly is the problem? Whereas member states preferred to define the problem narrowly in terms of hate speech and hate crimes, supra- and transnational actors defined the problem more broadly to include racial, ethnic, and religious discrimination. Second, who should take action to address the problem? Answers to this question derive from one's interpretation of who *could* take action. Supra- and transnational actors sought to shift responsibility for this emerging policy area to the EU, claiming that the Union possessed competency to act under existing Treaty provisions. Although amenable to using supranational forums to denounce racism and xenophobia, member states rejected this claim and argued that European policy action could only proceed on the basis of a Treaty amendment. Answers to these two questions shaped each actor's response to the final question—what policy action should be taken? Member states preferred intergovernmental cooperation and coordination of national policies against racist speech and violence, whereas the EP and transnational actors supported a European Directive that addressed racial discrimination in addition to racist speech and violence. This section provides an overview of the radical right's resurgence, and through an analysis of supranational actions and member states' responses, it illustrates the divergent ways in which EU institutions, transnational human rights activists, and member states answered the foregoing questions.

4.3.1 A Resurgent Radical Right

At the EP's 1984 elections, 16 members of radical right political parties were elected to sit in Strasbourg. The *Front National* (FN) sent ten members, including Jean-Marie Le Pen; the remainder belonged to Italy's neo-fascist *Movimento Sociale Italiano* (MSI), which had increased its representation from four in 1979 to five, and Greece's *Ethniki Politiki Enossis*, which returned its single member. As a result of this performance, the radical right was able to establish the Group of the European Right in the EP, thereby gaining substantial financial support and political legitimacy. In 1989, Germany's *Republikaner* (REP) party won 7.1 percent of the vote in elections for the EP while the FN increased its vote slightly from 11.2 percent in 1984 to 11.7 percent in 1989 (Givens 2005). At this point, Britain's first-past-the-post electoral system effectively ruled out seats for any extreme parties.[2]

The FN also fared well in French elections for domestic office. The party won 9.7 percent of the vote in France's national parliamentary elections in 1986 and a temporary switch to proportional representation led to the party winning 35 seats in the French Assembly. The rules were returned to first past the post in the 1988 election, and the FN was unable to win any seats despite receiving 9.7 percent of the vote again. At the 1993 election, the FN improved to 12.4 percent of the vote; however, they did not win any seats. Le Pen received 14.4 percent of the vote in the first round of the 1988 French presidential election, but did not make it into the second round (Givens 2005).

In Germany, the *Republikaner* and the *German People's Union* (DVU) performed well in a series of state and local elections during the 1980s and early 1990s. Historically, the *Nationaldemokratische Partei Deutschlands* (NPD) had been the main party on the extreme right in Germany, winning as much as 4.3 percent of the vote in the 1969 *Bundestag* elections. The REP, established in 1983, was initially led by a former Waffen-SS officer, and campaigned on a "strong antiforeigner theme" (Conradt 2005: 113). At the 1989 West Berlin election, the REP campaigned heavily on the issue of immigration and took 7.5 percent of the vote (Kitschelt 1995: 218–20). Three years later and after the fall of the Berlin Wall, the REP won 10.9 percent of the vote in the state of Baden-Württemburg, winning a block of seats and a foothold in an important state. The CDU was particularly affected by the REP's success, losing voters at twice the rate of the *Sozialdemokratische Partei Deutschlands* (SPD) (Kitschelt 1995: 233). The DVU was formed in 1987 in Bavaria, and had some minor success at the state level. The party went on to join with the NPD for state elections in the former East Germany.

France and Germany were not the only countries to experience a resurgent radical right. Austria's Freedom Party saw consistent gains after Jörg Haider took over control of the party in 1986. It began to challenge the mainstream parties during the 1990s, culminating in the party winning over 27 percent of the vote in the 1999 legislative election and joining a coalition with the conservative People's Party. Although the FPÖ was only able to contest European Parliament elections after 1995, the year in which Austria abandoned its post-World War II neutrality and joined the EU, the FPÖ's success still influenced Europe's deliberations over xenophobia and racism (Givens 2005).

4.3.2 Glyn Ford

Glyn Ford started his political career as a Labour Party councillor for Manchester in 1978, having stood two years earlier, but not winning the seat at that time. He had been active in Labour Party politics with his parents before then, came from a working-class background and was the first in his family to finish college. He was very aware of the emergence of the British National Front (NF), particularly after their relative success in the by-election in West Bromwich, where they polled 16 percent of the vote.

Ford became active with the Anti-Nazi League, which confronted NF marches with counter-demonstrations, and discouraged landlords from renting space to NF for meetings. The NF was seen as a new generation of neo-Nazis, and they were known for attacks on people of color. In 1974 they fielded 54 candidates in the parliamentary election, but none were able to gain a significant percentage of the vote.

Ford was elected to the European Parliament in June of 1984, an election in which Jean-Marie Le Pen's FN won ten seats. A small group of neo-fascists had already formed a small parliamentary group, including the Italian MSI, led by Georgio Almirante, a Greek from a pro-generals party, EPEN, and the Vlaams Blok from Belgium. After the 1984 election they formed an official political group in the parliament called the "Technical Group of the European Right."

The Socialist parliamentary group felt it was important to take some kind of action against the far right. Ford found the rule that allowed the creation of a Committee of Inquiry, and collected the required number of signatures from the left that would allow them to look into racism and fascism in Europe. All parliamentary groups were required to nominate members, but Le Pen's group refused to make a nomination. In the end they did nominate a member, after it was clear the inquiry would move forward.

From the time the European Parliament became a relevant actor with direct elections in 1979 until 1984 there had been only one parliamentary question on racism. However, Ford's use of the Committee of Inquiry within the Parliament played an important role in setting the agenda, and putting racism on the agenda for the European Parliament for the foreseeable future.

It is clear that British discourses around race relations, anti-racism, and anti-fascism had an impact on Glyn Ford's approach to the rise of far right parties in the European Parliament. In Britain, the mode had been to take quick action against "neo-fascists" like the NF. Glyn Ford merely moved this framing into the context of the European Parliament, taking advantage of institutional measures which had not been utilized in the past, developing a new repertoire of action, and drawing on discourses from the anti-fascism movements in Britain.

4.3.3 Europe Responds to the Radical Right

Four months after the 1984 EP elections, with impetus from Glyn Ford, Parliament established a Committee of Inquiry to examine the "Rise of Fascism and Racism in Europe." This Committee was chaired by MEP Ford, but became known as the "Evrigenis Committee" after its rapporteur, Dimitrios Evrigenis, a Greek center-right politician who had a serious commitment against the authoritarian right. Some argued that the EP did not have the competency to deal with racism, but Ford rejected this argument, since this was not explicitly stated in any treaties. The Committee was ultimately created over the objections of Le Pen, by then an MEP (*Report of the Committee of Inquiry into the Rise of Fascism and Racism in Europe*, European Parliament 1985: 10–11, hereinafter "Evrigenis Report").[3] The Committee's terms of reference merit close attention. Rather than focusing on racial discrimination, the EP defined the problem in terms of fascism and racism, particularly the "growth and size of fascist, racialist and related groups within Europe." The EP charged the Committee with examining links between these groups and the potential causes of their proliferation as well as the policies employed by member states for combating these types of organizations (Evrigenis Report 1985: 11).

Over the course of its investigation, the Committee held hearings and interviewed a variety of key actors, including Harlem Desir of France's anti-racism organization *SOS Racisme*. Overall, the Committee spent two years collecting evidence. Hearings were held in several different cities, to bring in local activists and politicians who could provide direct evidence related to issues around racism and discrimination, particularly against Jews and ethnic minorities.

The Evrigenis Report pays relatively little attention to the phenomenon of racial discrimination and to national antidiscrimination laws as opposed to laws that target racist speech and hate crimes (Evrigenis Report 1985: 82–84). Despite its limited definition of the problem, among its 41 recommendations, the Committee encouraged member states to adopt several policies that related to discrimination—policies that we ultimately see embodied in the RED. These include establishing "effective means of legal recourse in disputes relating to racial discrimination" and guaranteeing NGOs a "right to institute

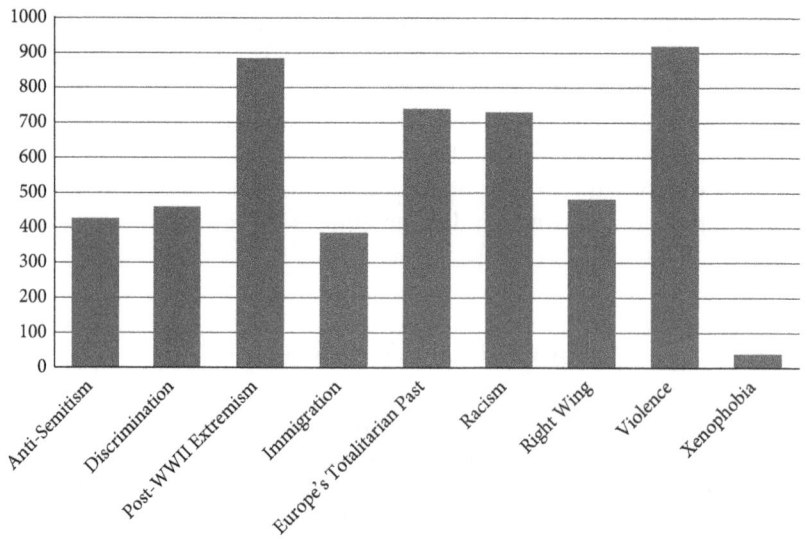

Figure 4.1 Evrigenis hearings

civil proceedings." It also recommended that the EU's powers and responsibilities in the area of "race relations" be defined "more broadly." This, the Evrigenis Committee suggested, could be accomplished in any of three ways: first, through a liberal interpretation of the TEU's existing provisions and the EU's implicit powers; second, pursuant to Article 235 of the TEU, which allows for an expansion of European authority, with the Council's unanimous support, in order to achieve an EU objective;[4] or "if necessary," through a revision of the TEU (Evrigenis Report 1985: 95–96, 104–105). An examination of the hearing documents and the Report shows a broad approach, with an emphasis on extremism, racism, and violence (see Figures 4.1 and 4.2).

In 1986, the Council realized one of the Evrigenis Report's recommendations by joining the EP and Commission in formally condemning racism and xenophobia by means of a Joint Declaration.[5] This measure also defined the problem narrowly, focusing on the "growth of xenophobic attitudes, movements and acts of violence" that are "often directed against immigrants" (reprinted in European Commission 1997: 12).[6] However, in contrast to the Evrigenis Committee, the Declaration virtually ignored the issue of discrimination—only its final sentence acknowledges a "need to ensure that all acts or forms of discrimination are prevented or curbed." Moreover, endorsing purely intergovernmental solutions, it neither committed member states to specific, domestic policy actions nor set forth a basis for the development of EU competency in this policy area. As the Council's first formal recognition of the problem of racism, this Joint Declaration is symbolically important. In

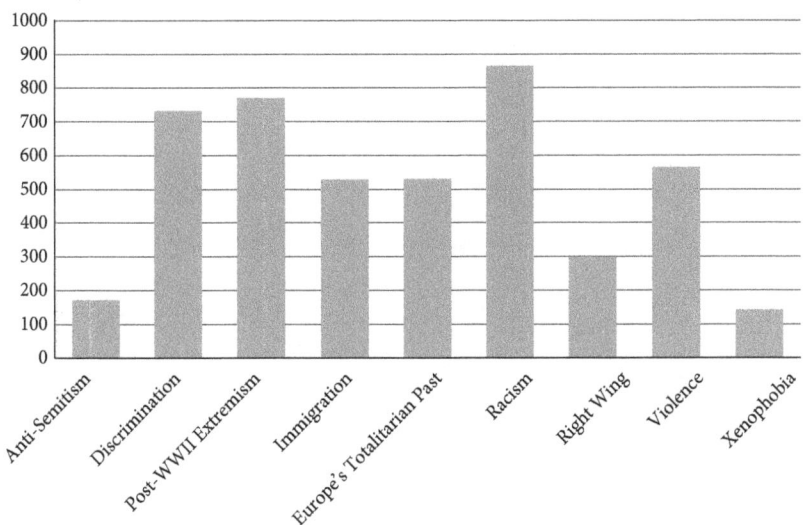

Figure 4.2 Evrigenis Report

substantive terms, however, it has been described as "a simple insipid document" that constitutes nothing more than a "false dawn in policy on racial discrimination" (German MEP Franz-Ludwig Schenk Graf von Stauffenberg, quoted in Bleich and Feldmann 2004: fn. 3).[7]

The European Commission and the EP nevertheless continued to press member states for more meaningful action on the issues of racism and discrimination. In 1988, the Commission submitted a proposal to the Council for a resolution on racism and xenophobia that would have encouraged member states to adopt antidiscrimination legislation where it did not already exist and enhance the effectiveness of existing legislation by revising definitions of discrimination and improving access to justice. Its proposal echoed policy recommendations that had appeared in the Evrigenis Report. Although the resolution was to be non-binding, it still took two years for the Council to reach agreement on a considerably weaker version of the Commission's initial proposal. As these negotiations dragged on, the EP convened a new Committee of Inquiry, this time with Glyn Ford as rapporteur, to produce a second report on racism and xenophobia.

The Council ultimately adopted a Resolution in 1990 that acknowledged that "acts inspired by racism and xenophobia may be countered by legislative or institutional measures," including antidiscrimination laws, authorizing NGOs the right to initiate or support legal proceedings, and the provision of legal assistance.[8] However, it did not obligate member states to take any of these actions, nor did it express support for granting the EU competency in this policy area. In fact, the Council annexed a declaration to the Resolution

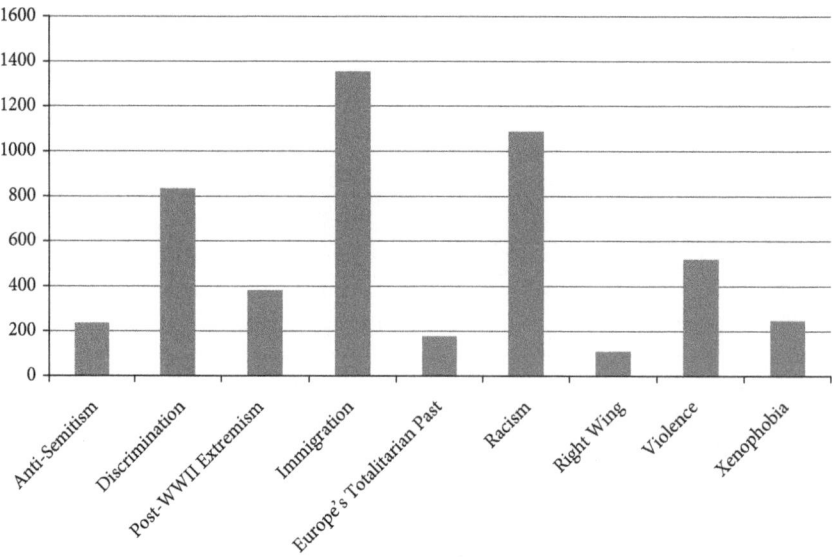

Figure 4.3 Ford Report

expressly providing that its implementation may *not* lead to an enlargement of the EU's competency as defined by the TEU (Ford 1992: 101). The following year, the EP released the "Ford Report." Among its 77 proposals, most of which focused on migrants and TCNs, it recommended that member states enact antidiscrimination laws "condemning all racist acts" and enabling "associations to bring prosecutions for racist acts or appear as joint plaintiffs" (Ford 1992: 59–60). These findings would be echoed in the Kahn Commission Report, as we will discuss in the next sections of this chapter.

The text analysis of the Ford Report (see Figure 4.3) indicates a continued emphasis on immigration and racism, as well as discrimination. There is clearly less focus on extremism and violence than in the Evrigenis Report, indicating an ongoing evolution in the discourses from antiracism toward antidiscrimination.

Following the dissemination of the Ford Report, the European Parliament would no longer play the main role in moving forward the antidiscrimination agenda. Although actors such as Glyn Ford would continue to be involved through the Kahn Commission and other venues, the Commission and the Starting Line Group would move the agenda forward through the passage of the RED.

The foregoing series of events is significant for at least three reasons. First, it shows the EP and the Commission using their agenda-setting capacities to put the issues of racism, fascism, and xenophobia on the European agenda. However, the Commission, more mindful of member state preferences, sought a non-binding, intergovernmental policy solution, whereas the EP advocated a supranational solution. These events also show the limits of supranational influence. The 1986 Joint Declaration and 1990 Resolution, both of which required member state approval, focus on the problems of racism and xenophobia, and they pursue strictly intergovernmental solutions. They therefore demonstrate the capacity of member states to assert their preferences over those of the EP and Commission.

Second, the EP's reports, in particular, illustrate the multiplicity and complexity of the problems facing European societies. They canvassed an array of policy areas, including immigration, citizenship, hate speech, violence, and discrimination, and thus they elicited a wide variety of policy recommendations. This made it difficult to generate and sustain momentum for any single recommendation or set of recommendations. Moreover, by addressing the issues of racism and discrimination within a broader discussion of migration and citizenship, European action in this area fell prey to the politics of immigration and political resistance to an expansionary conception of EU citizenship. The analysis of this point shows member states effectively containing the expansionary efforts of EU institutions. Yet, although the Joint Declaration and Resolution were essentially toothless instruments, their condemnation of racism, xenophobia, and discrimination and their commitment to the values of equality and non-discrimination rendered them potential resources for advocacy groups that might later seek to engage in "accountability politics" (Keck and Sikkink 1998: 98).

4.4 A NEW ACTOR EMERGES: THE STARTING LINE GROUP

A variety of organizations had been lobbying on behalf of migrants and racial and ethnic minorities in the 1980s. By the early 1990s, activists realized that the EU was being used to construct "Fortress Europe," a set of policies designed to act as a bulwark against immigrants and asylum seekers who had been coming to Europe in increasing numbers. This experience catalyzed them to look for other, more propitious means of advancing their interests in order to ameliorate the effects of restrictive immigration, asylum, and citizenship policies (Dummett 1991; Bell 2002: 68). Activists therefore reframed the problem as one of racism and discrimination (Chalmers 2000a). Having redefined the problem, a new set of solutions concomitantly followed. The enactment of anti-discrimination law, particularly at the EU level, became a priority, particularly after a group of activists and NGOs mobilized around this policy solution.

In 1991, a variety of activists and NGOs led by Jan Niessen, Secretary-General of the Churches' Committee for Migrants in Europe, a transnational NGO, coalesced into a loose transnational advocacy network that would call itself the "Starting Line Group." The idea for such a network was conceived at a meeting of lawyers, activists, and experts, including government advisers, a former member of the European Commission, and civil servants from six countries (Belgium, France, Germany, Italy, the Netherlands, and the United Kingdom). From the beginning, several organizations assumed a leading role, including the Churches' Committee, as well as Britain's CRE and the Dutch National Bureau against Racism, two quasi-state organizations that had been created for purposes of addressing issues concerning migrants and racial or ethnic minorities at the national level. They were subsequently joined by Belgium's Royal Commission on Policy towards Immigrants. Later, Niessen would form the Migration Policy Group (MPG), a Brussels-based think tank that after 1996 would serve as the group's coordinating body (Niessen 2000b: 502).

The main concern of the initial group that formed was the situation for TCNs in the EU. In particular they were concerned about a lack of protection from discrimination and limited freedom of movement. Only five out of the 15 member states had legislation on discrimination in the early 1990s. Also, with the prospect of new countries from Eastern Europe joining the EU, it was important to have legislation in place before accession.[9]

After careful deliberation, the organizers chose to draft an antidiscrimination Directive and develop a lobbying campaign around it (Dummett 1994: 530; Chopin 1999c: 111; Chopin and Niessen 2001). They accepted, as had been suggested in the Evrigenis Report, that the EU possessed the requisite authority under the TEU to adopt such a measure.[10] By 1992, the group had produced its proposal, "The Starting Line," from which the loose coalition of organizations took its name. This proposed Directive was translated into all of the languages of the 12 member states and disseminated widely (Niessen 2000b: 501). In addition, in 1994, a copy of the Starting Line proposal was reproduced in the publication *New Community* (see Dummett 1994).

The SLG satisfies the defining characteristics of a transnational advocacy network (Lutz and Sikkink 2001: 2; Keck and Sikkink 1998). Its members shared a progressive set of human rights values. All were concerned in one way or another with migrant interests, including the fight against racism and xenophobia. In addition, many of the leading figures in the SLG were lawyers (Geddes and Guiraudon 2004), and as such, their expertise and competence empowered them to make authoritative claims concerning complicated legal matters (Haas 1992). These lawyers "combined a strong commitment to anti-discrimination legislation with a high level of EU-related technical know-how" (Geddes and Guiraudon 2004: 7).

Prior to the SLG's establishment, there was "very little coordination of national and EU-level actors" working on behalf of migrants and against racism (Wallace 2000: 192; Gearty 1999: 351). Various groups and activists appeared before the EP's Evrigenis and Ford Committees, and two in particular, the

Brussels-based Migration News Sheet, which collected country-by-country information on racial discrimination, and the London-based Searchlight, which collected information on extremist right-wing organizations, assisted the Ford Committee in the production of its 1992 Report (Niessen 2000b: 494). Nevertheless, collective action was inhibited because most pro-migrant organizations saw the EU as a forum in which migrant interests were more likely to be undermined than advanced (Niessen 2000b). In addition, although a variety of anti-racism organizations existed across Europe, they experienced difficulty in focusing their effort and coordinating their activities (Ruzza 1999). The multiplicity of issues and policy priorities inhibited effective collective action.

The SLG surmounted these obstacles by devising a campaign that had a single focus—the adoption of an EU Directive against racial discrimination (Chopin 1999c: 111). According to Jan Niessen of the MPG, "we never wanted to be bothered by anything else—petitions, conferences—we focused only on legislation" (interview). By various reports, the coalition's membership eventually grew to include several hundred organizations, such as the Struggle against Racism; the Commissioner for Foreigners' Affairs of the Senate of Berlin; Caritas Europe; the European Jewish Information Network; the Migrants Forum; the European Anti-Poverty Network; and the European Roma Rights Centre, among others (see Dummett 1994: fn. 1; Chopin 1999c: 111; Niessen 2000b: 496). The MPG coordinated the network's efforts, and by design it rarely sought to convene the SLG as a group. According to Niessen, it was thought that members of the Group should "never" be brought together precisely because of their varied and potentially conflicting interests (interview). If the SLG were convened, the leadership feared that talk of other issues would potentially weaken the coalition.

The SLG's single-minded focus on a Directive also facilitated the practice of "accountability politics" (Keck and Sikkink 1998). The Council had expressly acknowledged the problems of racism and discrimination and endorsed the need for their eradication. By offering member states a specific, targeted policy solution, rather than an assemblage of myriad policies, as had previous EP reports, the SLG could pressure member states to take action. The SLG formally launched its Starting Line proposal in the lead-up to the European Council's 1992 Edinburgh Summit. Thereafter, references to the problem of racism regularly appeared in the Presidency Conclusions that were published after each meeting of the European Council between 1992 and 1997, but member states refrained from taking further action on the basis that the EU did not possess authority to adopt racial antidiscrimination policy under the TEU.

In addition, the SLG forged important relationships with both the EP and the Commission. Parliament endorsed the SLG's draft Directive in two resolutions, and explicitly asked the Commission to use the Starting Line proposal as a basis for drawing up a Directive aimed at harmonizing legal measures in the member states to eliminate racial discrimination.[11] These actions kept the proposal on the agenda and enhanced the credibility of the proposal as well as that of the SLG as a key player in this policy area. The Commission, by contrast, withheld formal expressions of support for the Starting Line and refrained from using its power to submit to the Council a proposal for such a Directive. Commissioners were divided on the issue of the EU's legal authority to adopt such a Directive absent a Treaty amendment. In addition, based upon the Commission's experience with the 1990 Resolution, they feared that member states would dilute or reject any such proposal and thereby make the Commission look weak (Chopin and Niessen 2001: 101). The Commissioners thus recognized the limits of their power vis-à-vis member states, and they did not want to get too far ahead of member states on this issue. In this way, they rationally anticipated the member states' response, illustrating the limits of their autonomy.

Realizing that insufficient political will existed within the Commission and among member states to rely on existing Treaty authority as the basis for a Directive, in 1993 the SLG shifted its strategy to seeking an amendment to the TEU that would expressly provide the EU with authority to adopt an antidiscrimination Directive on grounds other than gender (Commissioner Ruberti: Debates of the European Parliament No. 4-452/112, 26.10.94). This tactical adjustment proved consequential. Member states were on record denouncing racism since the 1986 Joint Resolution, yet the claim of insufficient Treaty authority provided a convenient excuse for inaction at the EU level (Wallace 2000). Securing a Treaty amendment would require the unanimous consent of member states, a particularly difficult proposition, especially so long as the Conservatives continued to govern Britain. Yet, just four years after the SLG released its Starting Point proposal, Article 13 was adopted. What happened during this period to produce such an unexpected result?

4.5 THE ROLE OF THE RADICAL RIGHT

At its 1994 meeting in the Greek city of Corfu, the European Council acted on a proposal by the French and German governments and established the Kahn Commission. This Commission ultimately recommended that the TEU be amended to assign the EU competency over racial antidiscrimination policy, and it played a key role in setting the agenda for the 1996–1997 IGC at which Article 13 was adopted. The Kahn Commission's creation set the stage for the Europeanization of antidiscrimination policy, and indicated a major shift in the discourses from anti-racism to antidiscrimination as indicated in our analysis in Chapter 2.

In creating the Kahn Commission, the European Council acted at the initiative of the governments of French President François Mitterrand and German Chancellor Helmut Kohl, thus seemingly validating an intergovernmental explanation (Geddes 2000). Scholars suggest French and German preferences were transformed by perceived threats from the radical right (Wallace 2000: 153–97). The success of right-wing parties prompted responses from mainstream parties at the national level, with the left supporting groups like *SOS Racisme* in France (Bleich 2003). Although politicians on both sides rejected the racism of the radical right, the conservative right parties in each country did pursue tougher immigration controls. The 1994 Franco-German proposal, however, was drafted *before* elections to the EP demonstrated the appeal of extreme right parties with aggressively anti-foreigner views to many parts of the community.[12] According to contemporary news reports, the creation of the Kahn Commission "was brought together as a device to sideline the issue during their [Kohl and Mitterrand's] election campaigns" and "had originally been seen as a public relations ploy before the German and French elections" (Carvel 1994). However, the Commission was seen to have come through with "A serious strategy to combat racism in the European Union" (Carvel 1994).

A perceived threat from right-wing extremists did not necessarily induce the French and German governments to seek to Europeanize racial *anti-discrimination* policy. Such laws would have been novel in both France and Germany at the time, and they could be criticized for interfering in the private sphere, particularly in Germany where the Basic Law delineates and protects individual autonomy in the private realm.[13] By contrast, the Europeanization of policies against racist speech, violence, and organizations could prove politically useful to national governments for a variety of reasons. These include legitimizing the government's suppression of civil liberties in the name of combating right-wing extremism and providing national governments with a means of censuring their extremist opponents. As Adrienne Wallace (2000: 109) observes, racial violence, "which fell generally into the area of criminal law, allowed Member States to pose as champions of law and order as well as human rights without having to cede sovereignty in the areas of social policy, labor market policy, or migration policy."

During the early 1990s, right-wing extremism was on the rise in Germany. Following an improved showing in the March 1993 state election in Hesse, fears were expressed in the popular media that the *Republikaner* could surmount the 5 percent threshold at the following year's election and thereby gain seats in the *Bundestag* (Doyle 1993). The prospect of the *Republikaner* holding the balance of power led the CDU to declare that it would not enter into coalition with any group that threatened democracy (Doyle 1993). The German election was held on October 16, 1994, four months after the meeting in Corfu. Thus, the electoral threat posed by the radical right was certainly on Chancellor

Kohl's mind in the summer of 1994. Evidence exists to support the claim that Kohl wanted European action, or at least the appearance of action, on the issue of racist speech and violence. In the early 1990s, Germany experienced an escalation in racist violence against ethnic minorities and modest growth in neo-Nazi groups. For example, 17 people were killed and 2,500 were injured in a surge of racist violence in 1992 (Doyle 1993). In May 1994, the month before the meeting in Corfu, Kohl met leaders of Jewish organizations, including Jean Kahn, as "part of an ongoing round of talks on racist violence" ("German Jews tell Kohl of racism worries," 1994). His government introduced a bill that would strengthen Germany's criminal law against incitement to racial hatred in December 1994.[14] This corroborates the claim that Kohl sought to use the Corfu measure as "political cover for cracking down on right-wing racism at home" (Barber 1994) in order to strengthen his domestic position.

In 1994, France already had laws that criminalized hate speech and hate crimes so the Corfu proposal did not threaten to weaken its control over domestic policy. President Mitterrand's support for the proposed Commission probably derived from his assessment of the grim political situation at home. In March 1993, the right swept to power in the National Assembly, inaugurating a period of cohabitation with Prime Minister Edouard Balladur and the appointment of Charles Pasqua, a hardliner on immigration, as Interior Minister. Pasqua implemented many of the FN's immigration and citizenship proposals, rejecting only the most extreme (Simmons 1996: 106). Meanwhile, popular approval of the FN had declined. In one poll, 79 percent of respondents said they disagreed with the Front, and 73 percent agreed that Le Pen and the Front posed a danger to democracy, although 61 percent agreed with Le Pen's stance on immigration (Simmons 1996: 103, 105). In pushing for the Kahn Commission, Mitterrand probably sought to counterbalance the Balladur government. His support risked little political cost because France already had anti-racism policies in place, and public opinion polls indicated French discomfort with the hard edge of the FN's racist appeals. Mitterrand could thus safely assume that French voters would not punish him for a supranational effort against racist speech and violence. In any case the French were ultimately completely unaware of what was going on at the EU level and thought that antidiscrimination policy was a "gift from Chirac," and Germans were likely unaware of the policy coming from the EU as well. As Givens and Luedtke (2004) have shown, this area of policy is very low salience for voters.

4.5.1 The Kahn Commission's Mandate

The Council charged the Commission with making "recommendations on *cooperation* between governments and the various social bodies in favor of encouraging tolerance, understanding and harmony with foreigners" and developing "a *global strategy at the Union level* aimed at combating acts of racist and xenophobic violence" (European Commission 1997: 49, emphasis added). The precise meaning of a "global strategy at the Union level" is unclear and could encompass both intergovernmental and supranational action. Recourse to such ambiguous language derives from resistance among some member states. In this case, the Conservative British government was the most likely, but certainly not the only, hold-out.

In its original form, the Franco-German proposal would have assigned the task of developing this "global strategy" to EU institutions working with national governments rather than to intergovernmental negotiators, but this had to be changed in order to reach a final agreement among member states (Wallace 2000: 108). As a result, the Corfu initiative was ultimately "'placed under the 'third pillar' of the Union, with its work plan to be carried out…in closed meetings of national officials reporting back to Ministers'" and with "'no effective role for the European Parliament or Commission in these procedures'" (quoted in Wallace 2000: 108).[15] Wallace (2000: 108) infers from this that France and Germany intended meaningful supranational action, indicating an important change in the preferences of two powerful member states. Even if this inference is valid, however, the substance of the policy initiative was expressly tied to "combating acts of racist and xenophobic violence and incitement to racial hatred." Thus, France and Germany, with the support of the Council, continued to frame the problem in terms of racial *violence* rather than *discrimination* even though the Parliament, the SLG, and to a lesser extent, the Commission had been clamoring for action against discrimination for several years (European Commission 1997: 49; Barber 1994). Contemporary news reporting confirms this view. For example, one reporter characterized the Franco-German initiative as "one of the least contentious items" at Corfu (Barber 1994).

Initially, the Kahn Commission abided by its narrow mandate and refrained from considering EU legislative action or a Treaty amendment (Chopin and Niessen 2001: 102). However, it ultimately interpreted the problems of racism and xenophobia broadly and addressed "more sensitive issues such as job discrimination against ethnic minorities" as well as "incitement to persecution through the distribution of racist literature" (Carvel 1994). Although the Commission's final Report begins by framing the problem in terms of fascism, racism, and anti-Semitism, focusing primarily on hate speech and hate crimes, the Report ultimately refers to the problem of *discrimination* no fewer than 40 times in its 64 pages. As Figure 4.4 indicates, discrimination and racism are the two main discourses in this document. We explore the reason why this happened later in this chapter, but first we examine the member state response to the Kahn Commission's reports.

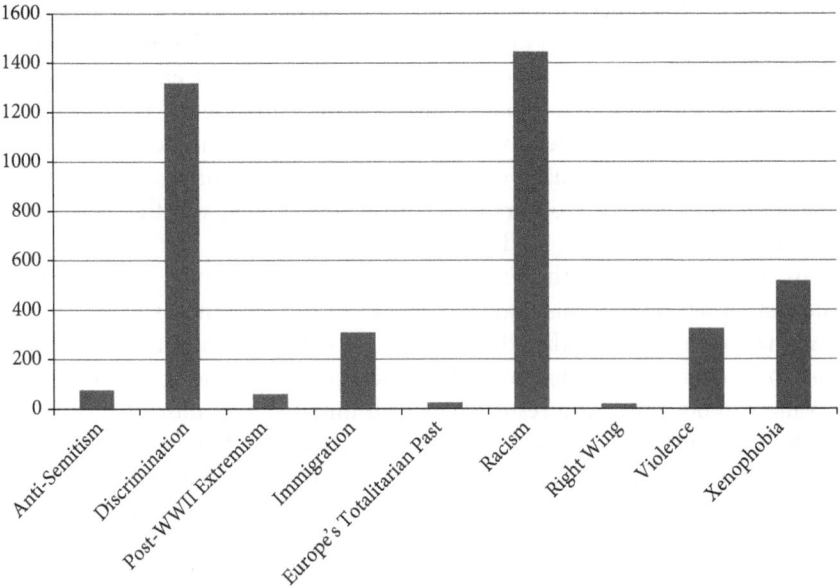

Figure 4.4 Kahn Commission Report

4.5.2 Member States and the Kahn Commission's Reports

The Kahn Commission issued several interim reports between November 1994 and its final Report in 1996 in which it recommended amending the TEU in order to give the EU competency to enact policy against racial discrimination. During this period, the Euro-skeptical Conservatives remained in power in Britain, thus providing a constant source of resistance, but national governments more generally did not support the Kahn Commission's recommendation. According to public accounts by SLG activists, member states generally "showed little interest" in taking a lead in this policy area (Niessen 2000b: 496).

A review of the Presidency Conclusions that were published after each meeting of the European Council between 1994 and 1996 reinforces this assessment. These Conclusions summarize the main issues discussed at the meetings and thus serve as an accurate barometer of member state concerns, particularly those of the governments that held the Presidency of the Council and thus chaired the meetings. They reveal a pattern by which the Council regularly acknowledged the problem of racism but issued symbolic gestures rather than substantive policy commitments. Even the June 1995 European Council in Cannes did not engage the interim report that had been issued by the Kahn Commission just two months earlier and in which the Commission proposed an amendment to the TEU (Wallace 2000: 122, 163–66). Instead, it

asked the Commission to "extend its work in order to study," in close cooperation with the Council of Europe, the "feasibility" of establishing a European
Monitoring Centre on Racism and Xenophobia (EUMC).[16] This is particularly
surprising considering that newly-elected President Jacques Chirac presided
over the conclave only a month after Le Pen received 15 percent of the vote in
the first round of the French election.

In October 1995, the Council adopted two Resolutions concerning racism
and xenophobia, both of which expressed ambiguous support for the Kahn
Commission's recommendations and clearly advocated an intergovernmental policy response. The first of these acknowledged the problem of employment discrimination but emphasized that policy action should occur within
the framework of the respective powers of the EU and member states. Thus,
instead of offering specific proposals for legally binding measures, it merely
urged member states to achieve a set of common objectives that includes
"guaranteeing protection for persons against all forms of discrimination on
grounds of race, color, religion or national or ethnic origin" and "fighting all
forms of labor discrimination against workers legally resident in each member
state."[17] The second Resolution focused on the role of education in combating
racist and xenophobic attitudes.[18] It neither recognized the problem of discrimination within the educational system nor espoused a binding, European
policy approach. At the June 1996 meeting in Florence, the Council approved,
in principle, the creation of the EUMC.[19]

4.5.3 Reassessing the Significance of the Kahn Commission

The foregoing analysis shows that the Kahn Commission's creation was the
product of short-term calculations. In this, its creation resembles the Council
statements that preceded it. Although the Kahn Commission was designed to
act primarily as an agent of the member states, it developed its own interests and
became a political actor in its own right (Moe 1990: 121). Thus, although the
Commission was initially unwilling to consider EU legislative action (Chopin
and Niessen 2001: 102), by mid-1995 it had drafted its own proposal for a Treaty
amendment. The SLG, we contend, played an important role in shaping the Kahn
Commission's discourses and persuading it to support a Treaty amendment.

The Kahn Commission created an opportunity for influence that was
exploited by both supranational institutions and transnational activists.
It created a new opportunity for the SLG to engage in information politics
and lobby on behalf of supranational policy action. The Kahn Commission
organized national roundtable discussions in member states with government
authorities as well as NGOs,[20] and the SLG participated in several of these
meetings (Chopin 1999b: 3–4). In December 1994 (two months after the Kahn

Commission began meeting regularly), the Group devised its own proposal for a Treaty amendment that it called the "Starting Point."[21] Jean Kahn, the Commission's chair, subsequently acknowledged the SLG's influence.

In addition, weeks after the Kahn Commission was established, the European Commission issued its *White Paper on European Social Policy* in which it suggested that "serious consideration" be given to introducing "a specific reference to combating discrimination on grounds of race, religion, age, and disability" at the "next opportunity to revise the Treaties" (European Commission 1994: 52).[22] It argued that this was necessary to realize free movement within the single market (Ch. VI, para. 27). Although the Commission resisted calls that it should use its right of legislative initiative to propose legislation, it adopted a Communication on Racism, Xenophobia and Anti-Semitism and a proposal for a Council Decision designating 1997 as the European Year against Racism.[23] Its 1995 Communication discussed the problems of racism and discrimination and finally called for the inclusion of a "general non-discrimination clause" in the Treaty.[24]

The Kahn Commission altered the political context in important ways. By having an intergovernmental body recommend a Treaty amendment (Bell 2002: 70), it became nearly impossible for member states not to reconsider their positions on a Treaty amendment, especially in light of the European Commission's new public position and the SLG's lobbying campaign. When member states initially refused to address the Kahn Commission's recommendations in a meaningful way, the SLG publicly criticized the Council for this (Wallace 2000: 126). The network was thus practicing "accountability politics" (Keck and Sikkink 1998). Moreover, the Kahn Commission's final Report was released in the lead-up to the IGC, at which the TEU was to be negotiated. The SLG argued that "failure to amend [the TEU] would be perceived as a setback for human rights rather than as maintenance of the status quo, now that the question has been raised by the European Commission itself."[25] By not amending the Treaty, member states would look like they were not interested in taking action at the IGC, particularly in light of a rising radical right. Member states realized that they could not refrain from taking some action on discrimination. Although they may have been in a strong position to maximize their interests in creating the Kahn Commission, in so doing, member states ended up fundamentally transforming the political context and their own positions.

4.6 THE 1996–1997 INTERGOVERNMENTAL CONFERENCE

The TEU that had been signed at Maastricht in 1992 provided for the Treaty to be revised four years later. Accordingly, an IGC was convened in Turin on March 29, 1996, which, under the successive Presidencies of Italy, Ireland,

and the Netherlands, oversaw the drafting of a new Treaty. The Treaty of Amsterdam was adopted by the European Council in June 1997 and signed by member states four months later. The IGC presented a unique opportunity for supranational action on antidiscrimination policy. The Kahn Commission's reports, the SLG's activities, and the European Commission's activities had all contributed to a "crescendo of voices" in support of an amendment to the Treaty (Bell 2001: 82). Further, the European Commission and EP also encouraged NGOs to participate in the IGC and particularly to submit proposals concerning racism and antidiscrimination (Hix and Niessen 1996). As a result, racial discrimination, which had "failed to be a central issue before 1996" (Hix and Niessen 1996: 10), was clearly on the IGC agenda.

The SLG coordinated lobbying efforts on behalf of the Starting Line proposal in the year before the IGC opened. To this end, it cooperated with local NGOs to organize a series of information seminars in the capitals of most member states (see Laflache 1998: 5). These seminars were intended to generate greater awareness of the IGC and the opportunity that it offered. From these national seminars there emerged an informal network that exchanged information concerning policy developments in the field of antidiscrimination, with particular emphasis on the positions that national governments could be expected to take at the IGC (Chopin and Niessen 1998). At the SLG's request, Simon Hix of the London School of Economics monitored the IGC negotiations. From the start, member states, with the exception of Britain, had agreed in principle to a Treaty amendment that would assign the EU competency over racial antidiscrimination policy (Hix and Niessen 1996: 59). Another critical development was the result of the May 1997 British election, where Tony Blair's New Labour replaced the Euro-skeptical Conservatives at the negotiating table.

The process of drafting a Treaty amendment raised several highly contentious and consequential issues. Based upon the ways in which these were resolved, any such amendment risked turning into yet another symbolic measure that produced no discernible policy change. Indeed, this was the outcome preferred by most member states. Here we show that member states were able to use their privileged position in the IGC negotiations to tailor what could have been, but ultimately was not, a weak Treaty amendment, over the objections of the SLG and the EP.[26]

The first issue concerned the nature of the Treaty amendment. Specifically, would it consist merely of a general statement that condemned racism, xenophobia, and discrimination, or would it actually accord the EU competency to take policy action? And, if the latter, what would be the ambit of this new authority? In other words, would it be limited to areas in which the EU already possessed authority to act, or would it constitute a new grant of authority that extended beyond the existing parameters of the EU's power? Although most member states supported a general Treaty clause that would condemn racism and prohibit racial discrimination, they were reluctant to add a specific clause that would expand the EU's competence in this area (Chopin 1999b: 1;

Wallace 2000: 140). By contrast, the SLG wanted to add a new article that would expressly assign the EU competency to legislate against discrimination. Ultimately, the choice of language used in Article 13 provided an uncertain outcome.[27] Its section 1 provides:

> Without prejudice to the other provisions of this Treaty and *within the limits of the powers conferred by it upon the Community*, the Council, acting unanimously on a proposal from the Commission and after consulting the European Parliament, may take appropriate action to combat discrimination based on sex, racial or ethnic origin, religion or belief, disability, age or sexual orientation. (Article 13, TEU)

Rather than definitively resolving the issue one way or the other, however, the italicized language actually had the effect of confusing the matter further and rendering Article 13's meaning ambiguous (Guild 2001: 67; Bell 2001: 82, 87–95; Griller et al. 2000: 160).

As an illustration of the complex legal issues involved, law professor Mark Bell (2000a: 87–95) devotes nine pages to identifying the various arguments that support an expansive versus a restrictive interpretation of the scope of authority conferred by Article 13. These arguments draw upon inferences from the Article's language, the Treaty's structure, ECJ precedents, and the wording employed in non-English versions of the Treaty. Bell ultimately concludes that a more limited conception of Article 13's scope is supported; thus, it "may be relied upon to prohibit discrimination *within those areas for which the Community already has competence*" (2000a: 95; see also Whittle 1998: 53). According to his interpretation, then, new legislation based on Article 13 would have to show that its area of application is already within the EU's competency. This would be easier to demonstrate with regard to antidiscrimination policy that targeted employment and education but not with regard to housing. The foregoing discussion illustrates the critical role of legal experts in the antidiscrimination policy area, and it highlights the potential for confusion and conflicting understandings of the final amendment's language.

The second main issue concerned whether the new Treaty language would require the adoption of European antidiscrimination policy or merely create discretion for the EU to act. Ultimately, Article 13 did not require that the Council take action pursuant to this new authority. This was an important element for the member states because without further action, Article 13 was merely another symbolic gesture. The third issue concerned the decision-making process through which any subsequent antidiscrimination policy would be formulated. According to the SLG's proposal, EU legislation would have been adopted by qualified majority voting (Chopin 1999b: 3), but here, too, member states weakened the amendment. Article 13 provides that the Council can only take action with unanimous consent, thus creating the possibility that a single obstructionist state could thwart policy action. Although "the general trend in the Treaty was to extend to the Parliament the right of co-decision on legislation," the procedure for which the SLG advo-cated, Article 13 nevertheless consigns the EP to a purely consultative role in the legislative process.[28] This was a surprising outcome given the Parliament's prominent role in the area of antiracism and antidiscrimination (Bell 2001).

Fourth, would the new Treaty article exert "direct effect"?[29] When an article possesses direct effect, individuals are able to invoke it in national legal pro-ceedings and ultimately to appeal to the European Court of Justice, which had proven to be an ally (Cichowski 2007). Thus, the SLG's proposed article would have conferred an immediate benefit upon victims of discrimination through-out the EU. In other words, would the new Treaty article generate a right to non-discrimination that could be invoked in the national legal proceedings in the absence of national implementing legislation? The Kahn Commission, the SLG, and the EP had wanted direct effect (Chopin 1999a).

Finally, on what grounds would discrimination be prohibited? Because it was concerned with the plight of third-country nationals, the SLG wanted nationality included as a ground upon which discrimination could be prohib-ited.[30] The Kahn Commission, too, had recommended that the amendment's protection against discrimination should apply irrespective of an individual's citizenship status (European Council 1995: 59). The Report, like the Starting Point, recommended application of antidiscrimination policy on grounds of nationality and religion. Ultimately, Article 13 transferred competency to the EU in the area of discrimination on grounds of sex, racial or ethnic origin, religion or belief, disability, age, or sexual orientation, but not nationality.

As Chopin (1999a: 4) observed:

> The confinement of Article 13 area of application to Community responsibili-ties has been subjected to differing interpretations. Some NGOs believe that, by amending the Treaty to give authority to institutions to adopt measures for com-bating discrimination, Member States have in fact broadened the Treaty's area of application. Furthermore, the general nature of this clause means that it may be problematic or delicate to use.

Article 13 was clearly the "product of political compromise" and differed in significant ways from the SLG's proposal (Chopin 1999a: 4). By weakening the Treaty amendment in the foregoing ways, member states believed that the action was not too costly. As the following chapter shows, however, they could not have been more wrong.

4.7 CONCLUSION

In this chapter, we have demonstrated that by the mid-1990s the resur-gence of the radical right had not yet convinced member states that racial antidiscrimination policy was warranted at the European level. Although member states repeatedly denounced racism and xenophobia, their statements concerning discrimination were ancillary. What was clear, however, was that the SLG and the Commission were having an impact on the discourses around the issue, ultimately creating a focus in the Kahn Commission on antidiscrimination. Moreover, to the extent that member states' proposals offered policy prescriptions, these resembled their own policies, and they did not resemble the policy prescriptions that are ultimately set forth in the RED. Article 13 satisfied these preferences in that it creates the possibility for action and gives member states something to point to so as to vouch for their liberal credentials and commitment to anti-racism despite their domestic shift to the right. Thus, when the road to Amsterdam is viewed as part of a historical process, "Although the member states remain extremely powerful, tracing the process of integration over time suggests that their influence is increasingly circumscribed" (Pierson 1996: 158).

The EP first placed the issue of racism on the European agenda, and between 1984 and 1997 it consistently called for EU legislative initiatives pursuant to existing Treaty authority as well as a Treaty amendment that would more clearly authorize such EU action. The Commission initiated European policy on racism in 1988, but member states balked and adopted a symbolic inter-governmental measure two years later. Perhaps learning from this experience, the Commission refrained from expressing public support for a Treaty amendment until 1994, after the Council had established the Kahn Commission. Moreover, it resisted calls by NGOs to use its right of legislative initiative to propose antidiscrimination legislation and thereby place the issue on the Council's agenda in the absence of a Treaty amendment. The Commission thus showed reluctance to get too far ahead of member state preferences.

Although the EP's Committees of Inquiry had performed a valuable function in documenting the problems of racism and discrimination, as temporary bodies, they proved inadequate for the task of mobilizing this information over the long haul. Moreover, the volume and breadth of the Committee's recommendations made it difficult to generate and sustain momentum for any single recommendation or set of recommendations. A network of transnational activists, by contrast, could continuously update information on the problems and national solutions.

NOTES

* This chapter was written with Rhonda Evans Case.
1. Press release IP/95/614, January 19, 1995, "Commissioner Flynn calls for European legislation to combat racial discrimination," London: European Commission.

2. The British National Party (BNP) and the United Kingdom Independence Party (UKIP) both contested the 1999 election, with UKIP winning seven seats with an anti-immigrant and anti-EU platform.

3. This Report became known as the "Evrigenis Report" after its draftsman, Dimitrios Evrigenis. We refer to it as such throughout the remainder of this book.

4. Article 235 provides: "If action by the Community should prove necessary to attain, in the course of the operation of the common market, one of the objectives of the Community and this Treaty has not provided the necessary powers, the Council shall, acting unanimously on a proposal from the Commission and after consulting the Assembly, take the appropriate measures." Following the Paris Summit of October 1972, recourse to this Article enabled the Community to develop actions in the field of environmental, regional, social, and industrial policy.

5. Joint Declaration by the European Parliament, the Council and the Commission against racism and xenophobia, June 11, 1986, OJ C 158, 25.6.1986.

6. In 1997, the European Commission published a single volume that reprints the text of key EU documents concerning racism. Throughout the rest of this book, we refer to this source rather than to the original documents themselves.

7. "European Union Anti-Discrimination Policy: From Equal Opportunities between Women and Men to Combating Racism, Directorate-General for Research" (Working document), Public Liberties Series LIBE 102 EN, accessed at <http://www.europarl.europa.eu/workingpapers/libe/102/text1_en.htm#B_6_>.

8. Resolution of the Council on the Fight against Racism and Xenophobia, May 29, 1990 (OJ C 157, 27.6.1990).

9. Interview with Isabelle Chopin and Janet Cormack, June 21, 2004, Migration Policy Group Headquarters, Brussels.

10. This argument rests upon Article 308 (formerly Article 235). However, Article 308 did not explicitly empower the EU to act with regard to racial discrimination, but rather it authorized the EU to take actions not explicitly authorized in the Treaty if such action is proven "necessary to attain, in the course of the operation of the common market, one of the objectives of the Community."

11. European Parliament, Resolution on Racism and Xenophobia, December 2, 1993; European Parliament, Resolution on Racism, Xenophobia and Anti-Semitism, October 27, 1994; European Parliament, Resolution on Racism, Xenophobia and Anti-Semitism, April 27, 1995; European Parliament, Resolution on Racism, Xenophobia and Anti-Semitism, October 26, 1996; European Parliament, Report of the Committee of Civil Liberties and Internal Affairs on the Communication of the Commission on Racism, Xenophobia and Anti-Semitism and on the Proposal for a Council Decision Designating 1997 as European Year against Racism, April 26, 1996.

12. The *Republikaner* received 4.4 percent of the vote in the 1994 EP elections.

13. For more on this element of the Basic Law, see Chapter 7 on the RED's transposition.

14. The German Criminal Code contains the offense of Incitement to Racial Hatred or Violence ("Volksverhetzung," § 130 Strafgesetzbuch—StGB, enacted in 1960), an offense substantially revised in 1985 and in 1994.

15. Its membership included one member state representative appointed by each national government (as well as those that were in the process of applying for EU membership), one representative from the European Commission, and two MEPs,

including Glyn Ford who had previously advocated European action on the problems of racism and discrimination.

16. Presidency Conclusions of the European Council, Cannes, June 26–27, 1995 (para.
5), at <http://www.consilium.europa.eu/ueDocs/cms_Data/docs/pressData/en/ec/
00211-C.EN5.htm>, accessed January 30, 2009.

17. Resolution of the Council on the Fight against Racism and Xenophobia in the
Fields of Employment and Social Affairs, October 5, 1995 (OJ C 296, p. 13,
10.11.1995).

18. Resolution on the Response of Educational Systems to the Problems of Racism
and Xenophobia (OJ 1995 C 312/1).

19. Presidency Conclusions of the European Council, Florence, June 21–22, 1996,
at <http://www.consilium.europa.eu/ueDocs/cms_Data/docs/pressData/en/ec/
032a0002.htm>, accessed January 30, 2009.

20. European Council Consulatative Commission on Racism and Xenophobia, *Final
Report*, Ref. 6906/1/95 Rev 1 Limite RAXEN 24 (General Secretariat of the Council
of the European Union, 1995), p. 3.

21. Starting Point 1994, <http://www.europarl.europa.eu/hearings/19951018/igc/
doc48a_en.htm>.

22. Commission, *European Social Policy—A Way Forward for the Union*, COM (94)
333 final, 27.7.94.

23. European Commission, Communication on Racism, Xenophobia and
Anti-Semitism. Commission Communication COM (95) 653 final; European
Commission, Proposal for a Council Decision Designating 1997 as the European
Year against Racism, Brussels, December 13, 1995, COM (95) 653. The proposal
was adopted by the Council of Ministers 23/07/1996 C237.

24. Commission, Communication on Racism, Xenophobia and Anti-Semitism, COM
(95) 653 final, 13.12.95, p. 18.

25. Available at <http://www.europarl.europa.eu/hearings/19951018/igc/doc48a_
en.htm#11>, accessed September 11, 2012.

26. National governments and NGOs alike advanced a flurry of specific proposals (see
Wallace 2000: 113–19), but we limit our focus to two sets of proposals. We examine those that were advanced by the Presidency because they capture member
states' positions more generally and because they ultimately shaped the outcome
in important ways. And, we examine the SLG's proposal because it represents a
more ambitious amendment, and because many of the groups that advanced additional proposals were also part of the SLG.

27. For a more detailed analysis of the legal issues, see Griller et al. (2000: 31); Guild
(2001: 65); Bell (2001: 85).

28. "European Union Anti-Discrimination Policy: From Equal Opportunities
between Women and Men to Combating Racism," Directorate-General for
Research Working document Public Liberties Series, LIBE 102 EN (Chapter 1),
accessed at <http://www.europarl.europa.eu/workingpapers/libe/102/text1_en.
htm#N_13_>.

29. The ECJ endorsed the position that it does not exert direct effect in *Grant
v. South-West Trains* [1998] IRLR 206, para. 48.

30. See Yu and Chopin (2001: 5–6).

5

From Discourses to Institutionalization: The Racial Equality Directive*

This legislation sends the strongest signal to Jörg Haider (leading light of Austria's Freedom Party), David Irving (the Second World War historian) and every thug who commits a racist crime on Britain's streets. With this new legislation Europe will reject race discrimination in any form.

Richard Howitt, Labour MEP for eastern England[1]

5.1 FROM TREATY TO DIRECTIVE

Although the SLG had been influential in the adoption of Article 13 in the Treaty of Amsterdam, this did not necessarily mean that member states would agree to exercise this new authority and develop a European policy against racial discrimination, as the SLG had proposed. The SLG had helped to shift the discourses from a focus on anti-racism to a focus on antidiscrimination. However, as we showed in the preceding chapter, member states did not necessarily want a European policy on racial antidiscrimination, and in the Treaty negotiation process they secured an ambiguous Article that required unanimous member state support for any subsequent European action. With the variety of national policy approaches to the issues of race and racial discrimination, one could reasonably expect protracted negotiations and difficulty in reaching final agreement on a Directive. In fact, considering these difficulties, the Commission could have been tempted to pursue a less ambitious measure than a Directive, such as a set of Recommendations, a Green Paper, or an Action Plan. The Commission, however, released its proposal for a Directive in November 1999, and just seven months later, the Council of Ministers adopted the RED on July 19, 2000. No other Directive of comparable breadth and complexity has been adopted in such rapid fashion (Tyson 2001: 201).

In these circumstances, one might expect the RED to constitute a "bottom-down" outcome, representing a weak, lowest common denominator measure. Yet the Directive, which prohibits discrimination on racial and ethnic grounds, is broad in terms of its material scope. It not only applies to employment, but it also encompasses a wide array of settings that includes the provision of goods, facilities, services, and housing that typically involve private actors, as well as benefits and services provided by the state, such as social security, health, and welfare. In addition, the RED pays special attention to the issue of enforcement. It requires the creation of a national equality body and the adoption of rules that enable NGOs to provide legal representation to aggrieved individuals in the courts. The RED differs significantly from earlier gender equality Directives in terms of its scope and attention to enforcement. The following chapter problematizes the policy content of the RED and explains why these differences occurred. Here, we explain why, given member state resistance, the RED was adopted at all, and why it was adopted so rapidly.

5.2 THE ARGUMENT

Within the literature, scholars generally suggest that member states adopted the RED in reaction to the success of Jörg Haider's FPÖ in Austria's 1999 parliamentary election and its entry into a coalition government in February 2000 (e.g., Geddes and Giraudon 2004). These accounts, however, tend to overemphasize Haider's role. We argue that the Austrian election exerted this effect because it occurred in conjunction with a shift to the left on the European Council and the development of a well-organized and highly institutionalized transnational advocacy network which had created a critical shift in the discourses around antidiscrimination, particularly through involvement during the Kahn Commission and the fact that they had already been working with the European Commission on a Directive, with support from the European Parliament. As described in a European Commission working document, "The Parliament's lobbying has dovetailed with an increasingly well-organised NGO lobby on racism. The turning point in this respect may be identified as the creation in 1991 of the Starting Line Group" (European Parliament 1997: section 1.1) The eight-month period following the Austrian election constitutes a "critical juncture" at which it became possible for this network to encourage more sympathetic member states to take action.

It is during the mid-to-late 1990s that the second discourse we describe in Chapter 2 comes into play. The SLG and Commission would need to shift the focus from an anti-racism approach with the member states, to an antidiscrimination approach at the EU level. In this chapter, we construct an historical narrative that traces the reaction of key actors to Article 13's adoption and identifies key points in the European legislative process that culminated in the RED. The first step in this process involved the Commission's formulation of a proposed Directive based on the SLG's "Starting Point." It would take three critical factors to move from the Treaty amendment to the RED. The discourse (discourse two from Chapter 2) developed by the SLG had to be incorporated at the EU level. Not long after the signing of the Amsterdam Treaty in October, the Commission came out with a working document in December of 1997 which incorporated many of the ideas around antidiscrimination policy which would ultimately become part of the RED. The third and perhaps most important factor in shifting the discourses and agenda was the new UK Labour government's presidency of the European Council in January 1998 which called for a focus on fighting racism, and a shift to left governments in France in 1997 and Germany in 1998.

We begin this chapter by describing the ways in which the Commission's proposal resembled key elements of the draft Directive for which the TAN had been lobbying for years. We examine a key shift in the political make-up of the Council, with elections in Britain, Germany, and France leading to left governments in the most influential member countries. After the Austrian elections in 1999, it becomes clear that the transnational advocacy network exploited three factors—"time constraints," "asymmetrical access to information," and a "need to delegate decisions to experts" (Pierson 1996: 137–39; Moe 1984)—in order for member states to accept the RED.

5.3 AFTER AMSTERDAM: KEEPING RACIAL DISCRIMINATION ON THE EUROPEAN AGENDA

The Treaty of Amsterdam was signed on October 2, 1997, and in the wake of this event, a debate erupted over Article 13's scope. Its resolution had important implications for the type of action that the EU could take pursuant to this new Treaty authority. Some states, most notably France and Germany, asserted that Article 13 did not confer any new powers upon the EU and that the Article's scope was strictly limited to the Union's existing powers (Chopin 1999a: 7–8). They insisted that any action taken must comply with Article 5 of the TEU, which establishes the principle of *subsidiarity*. Article 5 purports to limit the scope of the EU's authority by providing that European institutions can only take action when action at the national level is insufficient or ineffective. It is generally invoked by member states as a tactic for avoiding European action. According to this interpretation, the Commission must, in other words, "show why and how it is entitled to act within a European framework" (Chopin 1999a: 6).

The adoption of Article 13 precipitated relatively little action among member state ministries. This is clear from accounts of key figures in the SLG who immediately turned their sights on member states, seeking to assess the prospects for an EU Directive. In 1998, for example, Isabelle Chopin sought interviews with officials within the interior and the justice ministries of EU member states. Officials in the interior ministries were reluctant to talk with her, in some cases even refusing to grant Chopin's requests for interviews. By contrast, Chopin found officials in the ministries of justice to be the most cooperative, but she found that they had devoted a "rather superficial" level of thought to Article 13 and that "no particular work" on Article 13 had been "undertaken at ministerial level in any Member State." Thus, although the prospect of a European antidiscrimination measure applying to employment appeared to enjoy the support of the majority of interviewees, implementation of Article 13 was neither "urgent" nor a "high priority" (Chopin 1999a: 10–11). Surprisingly, the SLG observed reluctance if not hostility even among those member states that already had antidiscrimination legislation in place (Chopin and Niessen 2001: 104). However, some officials did suggest, as an alternative to pursuing action under Article 13, that measures should be pursued under the new Article 29, which recognizes the need for supranational cooperation among member states with regard to racism as a criminal act or offense.[2] Based upon its fieldwork, the SLG concluded that member states were "unlikely" to "take the lead in pressing for or strongly supporting a Commission initiative to that effect" (Chopin 1999a: 15).

However, anti-racism remained on the agenda in part because 1997 had been designated the "European Year against Racism"—the UK government was a strong supporter and held many events through its Commission for Racial Equality. Mike O'Brien was the new Labour government's Immigration Minister in the Home Office from 1997 to 2001. He was responsible for coordinating the government's efforts during the European Year against Racism. In a press briefing, he noted that "The European Year officially ends in December but many of the projects which the Home Office is now funding will carry on into 1998. The Prime Minister has decided that the concept of anti-racism will continue into the UK Presidency of the European Union from January to June next year."[3]

The UK did indeed make anti-racism a top priority during their six-month Presidency in 1998, along with issues such as fighting organized crime. Home Secretary Jack Straw told the press in January of 1998, "I also see the Presidency as a valuable opportunity for following up the European Year Against Racism 1997. We want to build on progress in the EU against racism and xenophobia, in particular, by convening a UK seminar on race relations."[4] The Labour government was clearly willing to take a leadership role in this area, again bringing its own concept of anti-racism and race relations to the EU level, as Glyn Ford had done with the European Parliament in the 1980s and early 1990s.

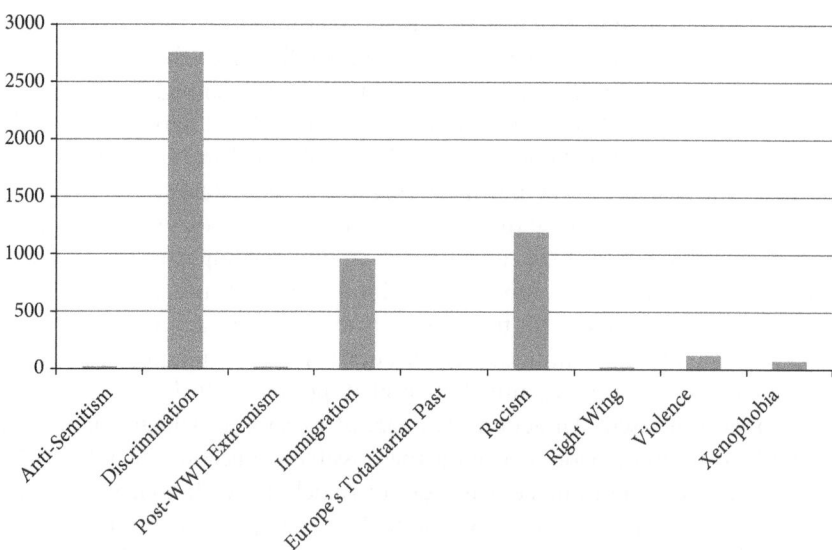

Figure 5.1 European Parliament Antidiscrimination Working Document

The Parliament also continued its activity on the anti-racism front. As noted in the European Parliament working document on gender and antidiscrimination policy, despite a lack of action by the Council of Ministers, "*Undeterred, the Parliament kept up the pressure for action throughout the 1990s. For example, based on a proposal in the Ford report, an annual Parliamentary debate on racism was instituted, ensuring ongoing attention to this issue. Consistently, the Parliament has stressed the need for legislative action at the European level, to add substance to the numerous declarations of good intent*" [emphasis in original] (European Parliament 1997: section 1.1). However, the Commission working document also notes that "In recent years though, there has been a discernible shift in the approach of the Council, and a new preparedness to consider substantive policy commitments at the EU level" (European Parliament 1997: section 1.1). This document was also significant in that it lays the groundwork for a Directive, drawing on the work done by the SLG. A text analysis of this document indicates that by this time the shift to a focus on antidiscrimination policy was clear (see Figure 5.1).

After the Treaty of Amsterdam was signed, the SLG and the Commission began working, often in concert, to get a racial antidiscrimination Directive onto the EU agenda. The SLG quickly convened a series of meetings, bringing legal experts together to redraft its initial proposal for a Directive on the elimination of racial and religious discrimination. The new proposal was called the "New Starting Line," and it was officially presented at the British Presidency Conference on Racism in Manchester in June 1998. The European Parliament urged the Commission to consider the SLG's proposal as it drafted its own proposal (Niessen 2000a: 210). In addition, the SLG launched a campaign to shape the prevailing understanding of Article 13's meaning. In November 1999, seven months after the Treaty of Amsterdam entered into force, Isabelle Chopin of the Migration Policy Group (MPG) published an analysis of Article 13 under the auspices of the European Network against Racism (ENAR). She argued for a broad understanding of Article 13, asserting that it constituted a de facto extension of the EU's competency and thus encompassed the power to adopt measures aimed at combating discrimination in all areas.

At the closing ceremony for the European Year against Racism in December 1997, Pádraig Flynn, Commissioner for Social Affairs, announced his intention to propose a Directive aimed at combating racism. In March 1998, the Commission released "An action plan against racism," in which it launched its effort to promote wide debate on the possible application of Article 13.[5] It stated its intention to make "early use of Article 13, with a view to ensuring that concrete proposals are on the table for adoption before the end of 1999."[6] The Commission conducted consultations before drafting its final legislative proposals. This consultative process concluded with a conference in Vienna, December 3–4, 1998 at which participants discussed the measures that the Commission intended to pursue for Article 13's implementation (Europaforum 1999).

Austria held the EU Council Presidency for the second half of 1998, and although racism was not a priority, it did come up in the Vienna Council conclusions:

> The European Council underlines the need to combat all manifestations of racism, xenophobia and antisemitism, both in the European Union and in third countries. It emphasises the role of the Monitoring Centre on Racism and Xenophobia in this regard. The European Council invites the Commission to draft proposals for its Cologne meeting for measures to counter racism in the candidate countries and invites the Member States to consider taking similar measures inside the Union.[7]

By 1999 the EU was preoccupied with enlargement and the euro, but antidiscrimination would become a high priority after the 1999 Austrian legislative elections.

5.4 STRENGTHENING THE TRANSNATIONAL ADVOCACY NETWORK

According to Patrick Yu, who served as the SLG's chair from 1997 to 2001, the year 1998 was "the busiest period in Europe on racial equality" (Yu 2006: 15).

In addition to keeping a racial antidiscrimination Directive on the EU agenda, the SLG and the European Commission cooperated in strengthening the TAN's resources and institutional infrastructure. This was important because, as Isabelle Chopin of the MPG observed, national organizations "do not always have the means to keep themselves informed about European policies" and "sometimes experience difficulty in appreciating the importance of working at national level, in order to be able to reach the European level" (Chopin 1999a: 20). Therefore, developing a hub in the network was important. Also in the lead-up to preparing its proposals, the Commission played an important role in sustaining the momentum (required in order to keep the issue on the agenda) of the TAN by providing funding and support for meetings. These measures would prove important for both the negotiation of the RED and the subsequent transposition process.

In another important development, pursuant to a recommendation made by the Kahn Commission, the Council established the EUMC, located in Vienna, as an independent body of the EU.[8] The EUMC became operational in 1998.[9] It was charged with collecting data and studying the causes and consequences of racism, xenophobia, anti-Semitism, and related intolerance as well as devising strategies for combating racism and promoting the integration of migrants and ethnic and religious minority groups. In furtherance of these objectives, it created the European Information Network on Racism and Xenophobia (RAXEN). The EUMC held open calls for tender and contracted with national NGOs, which it called National Focal Points, who collected, and transmitted information for each of the EU member states. These National Focal Points, in turn, maintained their own networks with key players in the national field. The EUMC analyzed the data from the National Focal Points and published a variety of reports.[10] These reports enabled the SLG to wage its campaign for a Directive through engaging in "information politics" (Keck and Sikkink 1998).

A second institution, the ENAR, was founded by the Commission in 1998 and became operational the following year. From the outset, the ENAR's development was rooted in campaigning as an offspring of the SLG. The ENAR serves as an official consultative body on race issues within the EU, and it receives funding from the Commission as well as a variety of NGOs (Yu 2006: 15).[11] It has grown to represent more than 600 NGOs. Like the EUMC, it developed formal links to national-level organizations. ENAR established roundtables in each member state that formally connect the Brussels-based Network to national NGOs (Chopin 1999a). This structure allowed the SLG to collect and disseminate information as well as coordinate the lobbying activities of its far-flung network. For example, in conjunction with the Commission's release of its proposed Directive, Isabelle Chopin (1999b) published under ENAR auspices a strategic plan that explained the EU legislative process and outlined the SLG's main lobbying strategy. Similar strategic documents were published by other members of the TAN, including the MPG and Britain's CRE (Chopin and Niessen 2002).

Following the adoption of Article 13, the transnational advocacy network waged an information campaign in order to counter two main arguments that were being advanced by member states. The first argument was that racial and ethnic discrimination was not a significant problem. And second, even if discrimination were a problem, special antidiscrimination legislation was unnecessary and even redundant because member states already had national laws that provided for equal treatment. The SLG worked to demonstrate the existence of discrimination as a national problem across the member states, to illustrate the inadequacy of existing national laws, and to emphasize the value of special antidiscrimination laws and institutions. To this end, the MPG, the EUMC, and the ENAR published a variety of studies, and in some instances, they collaborated in their efforts. For example, the MPG and the EUMC undertook a project in which they compared the terms of the Starting Line and the Commission's proposed Race Directive with existing legislation in the 15 member states in order to demonstrate what member states would need to do in order to comply with the proposals (Chopin and Niessen 2000).[12] The SLG recognized that it was engaging in information politics. For example, in 2000, Jan Niessen published an article that commended "the role of policy oriented research" in NGO lobbying campaigns (Niessen 2000b).

In addition, with EU funding the MPG created new outlets through which to disseminate their information. In 1999, for example, it worked in conjunction with the Centre for Migration Law of the University of Nijmegen to launch the *European Journal of Migration and Law*, a quarterly journal on migration law and policy with specific focus on supranational developments in Europe. In its inaugural issue, Kees Groenendijk (1999: 7) justified the journal's creation. Among other reasons, he stated that the journal, "whilst adhering to academic standards," would offer "NGOs a platform for their ideas and, thus, could enhance their role in the making of new European migration law."

5.5 ASSESSING THE TRANSNATIONAL ADVOCACY NETWORK'S INFLUENCE

Because the SLG did not actually have a formal role in the legislative process, it had to exert its influence upon those actors that did, namely the Commission and member states. As we have shown, the SLG and the Commission enjoyed a symbiotic relationship—the Commission funded SLG activities and the SLG advocated for an expansion of supranational authority and policy-making. But what influence did the SLG have on the Commission's proposed Directive? Assessing the SLG's influence is significant for two main reasons. First, in contrast to expectations generated by liberal intergovernmental theories, it shows that societal interests can shape EU policy through supranational as opposed to national institutions. Second, as scholars widely recognize, "there is tremendous political power in the first draft" (Schattschneider 1960: 68). SLG representatives may not have been sitting alongside member states at the negotiating table, but as we will show, many of their ideas were present by virtue of their inclusion in the Commission's proposal.

Recall that the SLG had first drafted a proposed Directive in 1992, the so-called "Starting Line," after which the Group took its name. Although various elements of the proposal had appeared in the recommendations of earlier reports produced by committees of the European Parliament (Evrigenis Report 1985; Ford Report 1991), the Starting Line was unique in that it was the first such concrete measure to be proposed. Indeed, one law professor described it as "the most sophisticated, well-researched, and intelligent contribution" to the debate (Gearty 1999: 350–52). Because obtaining a Directive was the SLG's sole objective, it worked hard at publicizing the Starting Line proposal through a variety of means, including the circulation of briefing papers (Gearty 1999). Over time, it became the focus of much analysis by members of the SLG (Dummett 1994) as well as by independent scholars. Therefore, by the time that the Commission was preparing its proposed Directive, it knew that it would be compared to the Starting Line document. Indeed, Isabelle Chopin and Jan Niessen published just such a comparison in 2000 (Chopin and Niessen 2000).

The Commission's proposed Directive did not contain all of the SLG's preferred elements. The most obvious difference between the two documents lay in the fact that the Commission proposed two Directives rather than a single Directive as the SLG network had advocated. The "Race Directive" prohibited racial and ethnic discrimination in employment as well as other areas of public and private life. In this way, its scope far exceeded that of the earlier gender equality Directives that were limited to the realm of employment. By contrast, the "Employment Directive" prohibited discrimination on a wider array of grounds—religion or belief, disability, age, and sexual orientation—but its scope was limited to employment. The Commission calculated that the existence of "strong political will... to take action to combat as many aspects as possible of racial discrimination" increased the likelihood that a Directive with broad application could be adopted.[13] Therefore, it devised a separate, broader proposal that was limited to race and ethnic origins.

In addition, the New Starting Line and the Commission's proposal differed in terms of the grounds upon which discrimination would be prohibited. In contrast to the Commission, the New Starting Line also included religion as well as racial and ethnic origins. Chopin and Niessen (2000) criticized the Commission's proposal on its omission. The SLG wanted religion to be included in order to accommodate different interpretations and understandings of racism across member states and because of the difficulty in distinguishing between racial and religious discrimination (Chopin 1999b: 4). The inclusion of religion in the New Starting Line had, however, been controversial within the transnational advocacy network. Many religious organizations that belonged to the SLG feared that including religion would threaten the privileged position of their churches under national laws. In an effort to appease these organizations, the New Starting Line (Article 1.5), therefore, contained certain exemptions (Chopin 1999b: 5).

Nevertheless, as we show here, the two proposals resembled one another in significant ways. They did not differ significantly in terms of their material scope. Both were broader than the earlier gender equality Directives in that they applied not only to employment but also to goods and services, education, and a variety of state services. In fact, the scope of the Commission's proposed Directive exceeded that of the SLG's proposal in terms of employment and education, but it did not include welfare, housing, and the provision of facilities, all of which appeared in the New Starting Line. In addition, the New Starting Line contained two general clauses that extended the Directive's scope to include the functioning of "any public body" and "participation in political, economic, social, cultural, religious life or any other public field" (Article 1.2). The Commission's proposal contained no such provisions.

Compared to the Commission's proposal, the New Starting Line elaborated in greater detail the rights of victims and the need for appropriate and effective enforcement measures and judicial remedies. We emphasize three key differences. First, the New Starting Line provided that "any judicial remedy... shall include adequate compensation for both pecuniary and non-pecuniary damages" and further that courts shall not be limited in their ability "to award compensation or such other remedy as is provided for by national law" (Article 4b). Second, the New Starting Line obligated the member state to "provide support in respect of legal costs in accordance with the most favorable provisions of national law" (Article 4.c). The Commission's proposal contained no equivalent provisions. Finally, pursuant to the New Starting Line, NGOs would not only be allowed to provide complainants with support for their legal action, but they would also be permitted to institute legal actions in their own name and without seeking a complainant's approval (Article 4d). Key figures within the SLG emphasized the importance of NGOs in this regard (Chopin 1999a). However, the Commission's proposal limited NGOs to pursuing enforcement actions "on behalf of the complainant with his or her approval" (Article 7.2). Although the Commission did not incorporate all of the SLG's preferred provisions, its inclusion of provisions concerning enforcement is nonetheless important because earlier gender equality Directives did not incorporate such measures.

Both proposals included definitions of indirect discrimination. Although the precise terms of these definitions differed, each was rooted in a desire to make it easier for complainants to meet their evidentiary burdens in court (Tyson 2001). The Starting Line also included a provision that would have shifted the burden of proof from the complainant to the respondent where the complainant established a prima facie case of discrimination.

Despite the various differences between the Commission and the SLG's proposed Directives, both share important core elements. Although the Commission's proposal did not satisfy all of their preferences, the SLG decided to present the measure "as an acceptable compromise" so long as its "essential elements" were maintained (Niessen 2000a: 211). Based upon interviews with national policy-makers following the Treaty of Amsterdam's adoption, the SLG had concluded that member states were not likely to devise a stronger Directive (Chopin 1999c). In fact, the SLG concluded that member states would probably try to dilute the Commission's proposal. Therefore, rather than seeking a "better text" from the Commission, the network would instead pressure national governments to accept the proposal (Niessen 2000a: 211). To this end, ENAR published English, French, and German versions of a "campaign paper," written by Isabelle Chopin (1999b), that would assist "associated organizations" in stimulating "a well-informed policy debate at national levels" (Niessen 2000a: 211–12). As Paul Pierson (1996: 133) observes, "choosing which proposals to consider is a tremendously important (if frequently unappreciated) aspect of politics." By exercising its power of initiative, the Commission placed member states in a reactive position—the Council of Ministers was responding to a specific proposal rather than drafting their own *de novo*.

5.6 A CRITICAL JUNCTURE

The preceding chapter illustrated the ways in which radical right successes had precipitated action from member states. Here again, the success of a radical right political party required an EU response, but this time, the Commission used its agenda-setting function to put a Directive on the table. It released its proposal in November 1999, the month after Haider's Freedom Party won nearly 27 percent of the vote in parliamentary elections. Haider's success accelerated the time frame within which the RED was negotiated. Given the political context, particularly the fact that left governments dominated the Council, member states were more enthusiastic about the RED, in contrast to negotiating Article 13. However, since member states had not seriously considered implementing Article 13, most entered the negotiations with a relative lack of information and poorly developed policy preferences. In this context, the expertise of the EC and the SLG gave them an advantage in moving forward with the negotiations.

5.6.1 The Radical Right

In October 1999, the month before the Commission released its proposals for implementing Article 13, radical right parties stunned Europe by making dramatic gains at the polls in Austria and Switzerland. At Austria's October 3, 1999 parliamentary election, the FPÖ, led by anti-immigrant politician Jörg Haider, won the second largest number of votes. After protracted negotiations, it formed a coalition government with the Austrian People's Party in February 2000. Three weeks after Austrians went to the polls, Swiss voters reinforced perceptions of a rising radical right in Europe. Campaigning against the country's asylum policy and efforts to join the EU, the Swiss People's Party (SVP) won 23 percent of the vote, up from 15 percent at the previous election, making it the second largest bloc in the lower house of Parliament and undermining a longstanding power-sharing arrangement. Although Switzerland was not a member of the EU, these developments stoked fears among European political elites.

The EU responded to the FPÖ's electoral performance with unprecedented action, including a bilateral diplomatic boycott. At the time, the Council comprised of largely "left"-leaning governments, and all three of Europe's major powers were controlled by social democratic governments. In 1997, Tony Blair's New Labour had defeated Britain's Conservatives, and the *Parti socialiste* won control of the French National Assembly; the following year, the government of German Chancellor Helmut Kohl was replaced by a coalition of the SPD and Greens. Fourteen of the EU's foreign ministers threatened to isolate Austria if it let the FPÖ into government. Some national governments took especially prominent public positions against Austria. For example, Belgian Foreign Minister, Louis Michel, called for a boycott of Austrian skiing holidays.[14] The French and Belgian ministers made a point of leaving the room when Austria's Social Affairs Minister, Elisabeth Sickl, a member of the FPÖ, started to address an EU meeting.[15] In March 2000, a month after the coalition government was formed, Haider stepped down as the FPÖ's party leader, although he retained his position as governor of the province of Carinthia.

5.6.2 Negotiating the Racial Equality Directive

Discussions on the RED began on February 13, 2000, the very month that the FPÖ entered into a coalition government. The timing of these events created a perfect opportunity for the members of the European Commission and the SLG to shame member states into action on the proposed Directive. On February 4, the *Deutsche Presse-Agentur* quoted a spokesperson for EU Social Affairs Commissioner Anna Diamantopoulou: "'it is very important that given the current situation in Austria that the EU does not delay adoption of the Directives on non-discrimination on grounds of race.'" On February 24, 2000, Diamantopoulou called upon member states to adopt the Directives in response to the events in Austria. In the words of one unnamed EU official, according to the *Deutsche Presse-Agentur*, "adoption of the proposals 'are [sic] a test for how far we are prepared to go to turn our principles into reality.'" On March 13, 2000, in the midst of the negotiations, Diamantopoulou again invoked the message that adoption of the Directives would send in the midst of the Haider situation. "'To weaken these proposals,'" she warned, "'would send entirely the wrong message at this sensitive time'" (*Deutsche Presse-Agentur* 2000c).

According to Niessen (2000a: 212), the SLG believed that the Austrian situation created a favorable environment for the RED's adoption in two ways. First, it expected that Austria's new government "would not dare oppose the Race Directive out of fear that this would legitimize the reproach by the governments of the other fourteen member states that the Austrian government cannot be trusted because it includes a racist party." Second, if the other governments sought to oppose the Directive, "they would be blamed and shamed for not putting their political powers where their mouth is." The SLG considered this opportunity to be short-lived. Again, according to Niessen (2000a: 212), the blaming and shaming strategy could be employed only so long as the 14 member states maintained their pressure on Austria, a situation that the SLG estimated would "probably not last longer than one year." In addition, although it did not participate directly in the Directive's negotiations, the SLG did have indirect avenues of influence that it could exploit. Key network figures maintained close contact with the Commission during the negotiation process. According to Patrick Yu, he "worked very closely with the Commission and also gave legal advice or counter proposals to the Commission on certain issues that arose from the negotiation process of the Racial Equality Directive" (Yu 2006: 15). Moreover, from "conversations with the negotiators it became clear which obstacles were put in the way by which member states, leading to targeted and rapid responses at the national level" (Niessen 2000a: 212).

By the time of the RED's negotiations, there was little doubt that a racial antidiscrimination Directive would be adopted, but questions remained about its policy content. As one Commission official observed (Tyson 2001: 113), although "no member state was opposed in principle to the idea of Community law on racial discrimination, a number of Governments had serious difficulties with particular points." During the negotiations, important issues concerning the Directive's substantive content remained. As we saw in Chapter 4 member states were able to use their privileged position during the Treaty of Amsterdam's negotiations to ensure that a weak Article 13 was adopted. Even though the need for a Directive had been advocated by the SLG and the EP for years, member states had been slow to anticipate what a Directive would mean for them. This failure to examine the implications of EU action for their national systems, we contend, subsequently weakened the bargaining position of member states during the RED's negotiations, particularly within the context of the accelerated negotiation process.

Summaries of the negotiations show that member state negotiators were ill-informed, or at least less well-informed, than EU officials and SLG lobbyists about the precise meaning and implications of the proposed Directive's provisions. In fact, some "EU insiders" expressed doubt that member states "knew the full implications of what they were accepting" (Geddes and Guiraudon 2002: 350–51). In this respect, the RED's negotiations resemble those of the EU's equal treatment Directives that were adopted earlier. According to Hoskyns these Directives, too, were "passed without much awareness of their consequences" and interviews with national officials repeatedly showed that "those who negotiated the original provisions had no idea what force they would prove to have or the legislative upheaval they would provoke" (Hoskyns 1986: 306). Moreover, the practical effect of the rapid negotiations is reflected in descriptions of the process. According to Geddes and Guiraudon (2007: 135), the "negotiations were conducted swiftly, mostly in English, without translation of documents which saved time, and with phone calls to national capitals rather than references back that could take up to three weeks." Finally, the negotiations were characterized by their highly legalized nature (Geddes and Guiraudon 2002: 350).

In contrast to the negotiations concerning the Treaty of Amsterdam, in which member states had various options for weakening Article 13, in negotiating the RED, they had fewer options. One important negotiating point involved determining precisely where in the Directive to locate particular policy commitments. Directives typically consist of preliminary "recitals" that do not have independent legal value and do not create legitimate expectations (Klimas and Vaiciukaite 2008), followed by "articles" that contain the legal commitments. Recitals must be included in all EU legislation that does not require unanimity for its adoption; thus, they were *not* required in the RED, which did require unanimous support. As we show, inclusion of these recitals in the RED was driven by a need for "political reassurance" (Klimas and Vaiciukaite 2008) that emerged during the Council's negotiations and served as a key component of the bargaining process.

The Commission's proposal stated that

> indirect discrimination shall be taken to occur where an apparently neutral provision, criterion or practice is liable to affect adversely persons of a particular

racial or ethnic origin, unless that provision, criterion or practice is objectively justified by a legitimate aim which is unrelated to the racial or ethnic origin of a person or group of persons and the means of achieving that aim are appropriate and necessary.[16]

However, Britain and Germany, along with other member states, objected to the Commission's definition, arguing that it was broader than that of Directive 97/80/EC and, therefore, too broad. Negotiations over this provision lasted from early March through mid-May. The RED's definition of indirect discrimination ultimately eschews numerical references and instead states that such discrimination occurs "where an apparently neutral provision, criterion or practice would put persons of a racial or ethnic origin at a particular disadvantage compared with other persons, unless…"[17] However, to placate Britain, recital 15 was added to the RED, providing that national "rules may provide in particular for indirect discrimination to be established by any means including on the basis of statistical evidence" (Tyson 2001: 203–204). The compromise definition of indirect discrimination that appears in the RED allows, but does not oblige, member states to require the production of statistical evidence.

Member states were concerned about the Directive's implication for TCNs. According to the Commission's proposal, TCNs would be protected against discrimination that occurred on racial or ethnic grounds, but they would not be protected against discrimination based on nationality, nor would national provisions governing the entry and residence of TCNs and their access to labor markets be affected. This was provided for in a recital rather than an article. Member states debated whether the Directive should provide protection against racial and ethnic discrimination for TCNs, and they debated the more technical issue concerning where exactly in the Directive to locate this provision. Should the relevant language appear *only* within a recital, as the Commission proposed, or should it appear within *both* a recital and an article? Britain and Germany were particularly concerned about preserving national sovereignty vis-à-vis TCNs, but other member states as well as the Commission were very concerned about the "political signal" that this language would send if it were contained in an article. Ultimately, Article 3(2) provides that the RED "does not cover difference of treatment based on nationality and is without prejudice to provisions and conditions relating to the entry into and residence of TCNs and stateless persons on the territory of Member States, and to any treatment which arises from the legal status of the TCNs and stateless persons concerned." Recital 13 states that the "prohibition of discrimination should also apply to TCNs, but does not cover differences of treatment based on nationality and is without prejudice to provisions governing the entry and residence of TCNs and their access to employment and to occupation."

The RED addresses the issue of standing in a very opaque way. According to Article 7(2):

> Member States shall ensure that associations, organizations or other legal enti-
> ties, which have, in accordance with the criteria laid down by their national law,
> a legitimate interest in ensuring that the provisions of this Directive are complied
> with, *may engage, either on behalf or in support of the complainant*, with his or
> her approval, in any judicial and/or administrative procedure provided for the
> enforcement of obligations under this Directive [emphasis added].

The italicized language is sufficiently ambiguous with regard to the question of whether organizations may pursue the litigation in their own name. In addition, Article 7(2) provides national governments with discretion to establish rules by which it is determined whether an organization has "a legitimate interest" in ensuring compliance with the Directive. The precise nature of these rules could have the effect of precluding some organizations from sponsoring litigation.

During subsequent negotiations, however, Adam Tyson observed that "the precise status" of NGOs before the courts was "less important" to the Commission than was the issue of "access to support from a respected organi-zation" (Tyson 2001: 212). Such support, the Commission recognized, "greatly influences the ability of a complainant to win a case." Because some member states were troubled by the issue of organizational status, the Commission crafted, and the Council accepted, the compromise that appears in the RED (Art. 7.2). The language of Article 7 accords national governments some discre-tion in determining the criteria by which NGOs must demonstrate a "legitimate interest" in enforcing the law. By denying NGOs independent status as litigants and by requiring the complainant's consent to NGO representation, national governments were trying to thwart litigation rather than shift it to the courts.

The Commission had proposed that "Member States shall ensure that associations, organizations or other legal entities may pursue, on behalf of the complainant with her approval, any judicial and/or administrative proce-dure provided for the enforcement of obligations under this Directive" (Race Directive, Art. 7(2)).

> Member States shall ensure that associations, organizations or other legal entities,
> which have, in accordance with the criteria laid down by their national law, a legitimate
> interest in ensuring that the provisions of this directive are complied with, may pursue,
> on behalf of the complainant with his or her approval, any judicial and/or administra-
> tive procedure provided for the enforcement of obligations under this Directive.[18]

5.6.3 Remedies

The roots of the RED's language concerning remedies lie in ECJ jurispru-dence,[19] but it was the SLG that initiated its inclusion in the Directive. The

Starting Line (Art. 4(b, c)) provided that complainants shall be entitled to "an effective judicial remedy" and that "victims of racial discrimination shall be granted adequate compensation." The New Starting Line (Art. 4(b)) was even more specific, providing that judicial remedies shall include "adequate compensation for both pecuniary and non-pecuniary damages" as well as any other "compensation or such other remedy as is provided by national law." As adopted by the Council, the RED (Art. 15) states that "sanctions, which may comprise the payment of compensation to the victim, must be effective, proportionate and dissuasive."

5.6.4 National Enforcement Institutions

The European Commission's proposal (Art. 12(2)) provided that member states were obligated to establish "independent bodies" that were entitled to receive and pursue complaints of discrimination from individuals, to initiate investigations or surveys concerning discrimination, and to publish reports and issue recommendations on issues concerning racial or ethnic discrimination. According to Tyson (2001: 216), this proposal generated "a good deal of concern" both from member states that already had such bodies as well as from those that were unfamiliar with them. Many in the Council felt that the proposal had "overstepped the line between setting objectives and telling Member States how to achieve them" (Tyson 2001: 216). As a result, the Council watered down the provision requiring an "independent" body to oversee enforcement, and the RED merely

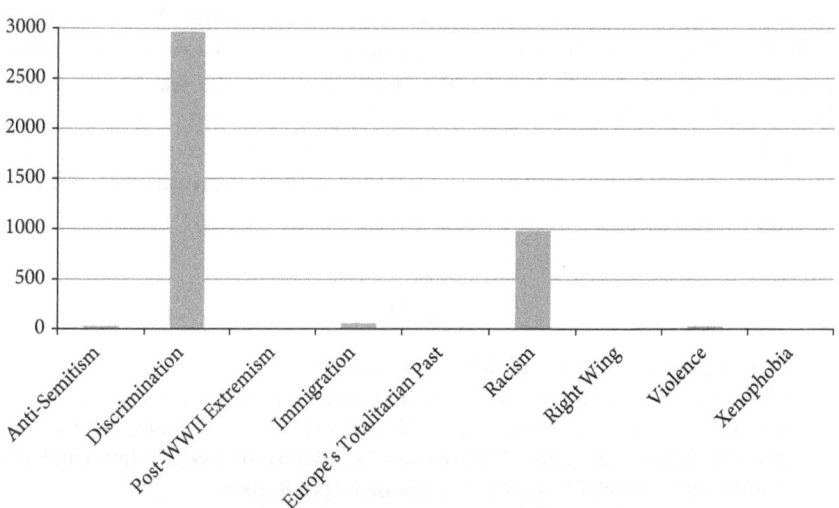

Figure 5.2 The EU's Racial Equality Directive

requires states to "designate a body or bodies for the promotion of equal treatment." Chopin (2000: 428) characterized this as "the biggest loss" in the negotiations.[20]

A text analysis of the final Directive indicates how the issue of discrimination became the dominant discourse, with issues such as extremism, violence, and even immigration falling away as issues (see Figure 5.2).

5.7 CONCLUSION

The processes through which the RED was adopted illustrate the importance of cooperation between state (here the EU) and societal actors. Early on, European institutions played an important role in disseminating information and analyses of a potential Directive (ECRI 1995; Bell 1998). The SLG gained a great deal of what it was hoping for from its early drafts of an antidiscrimination Directive.

However, member states shaped the terms of the RED in ways that would preserve their sovereignty or in ways that conformed to their existing domestic policies and political forces. There is some evidence of member states amending the Commission's proposal in ways that rendered the text more ambiguous, thereby providing them with greater discretion in terms of the RED's transposition. During this time period, Council negotiations were largely insulated from partisan politics and public scrutiny, a feature that provided national governments with greater flexibility and latitude.

In the next chapter, we examine the transposition and implementation of the RED. Many of the objections that were raised during the negotiations were raised again during the transposition process. This would impact timing of implementation in some cases, and ultimately, the way that the new laws would be implemented. The new century would bring major changes to the political landscape in Europe which would ultimately create a shift in the discourses around immigration, immigrants, and antidiscrimination policy.

NOTES

* This chapter was written with Rhonda Evans Case.
1. <http://www.lexisnexis.com:80/us/lnacademic/results/docview/docview. do?risb=21_T3466176916&format=GNBFI&sort=RELEVANCE&startDocNo=1 &resultsUrlKey=29_T3466176921&cisb=22_T3466176920&treeMax=true&tree Width=0&csi=138620&docNo=1>, accessed April 8, 2008.
2. Article 29 of the Treaty of the European Union reads: "Without prejudice to the powers of the European Community, the Union's objective shall be to provide

citizens with a high level of safety within an area of freedom, security and justice by developing common action among Member States in the fields of police and judicial cooperation in criminal matters and by preventing and combating racism and xenophobia."

3. <http://www.gov-news.org/gov/uk/news/european_year_against_racism_a_success/120.html>, accessed January 8, 2012.
4. <http://www.gov-news.org/gov/uk/news/tackling_organised_crime_racism_uk_presidency/35355.html>, accessed January 8, 2012
5. Commission, "An Action Plan against Racism," COM (98) 183 final, 25.03.98 at para. 2.2.2.
6. Commission, "An Action Plan against Racism," COM (98) 183 final, 25.03.98 at para. 2.2.2.
7. <http://www.consilium.europa.eu/uedocs/cms_data/docs/pressdata/en/ec/00300-R1.EN8.htm>, accessed January 8, 2012.
8. See Council Regulation (EC) No. 1035/97 of June 2, 1997 (OJ L 151, June 10, 1997) that was amended by Council Regulation (EC) No. 1652/2003 of June 18, 2003.
9. The EUMC was replaced by the FRA on February 28, 2007.
10. In March 2007, the EUMC was replaced by the European Union Agency for Fundamental Rights.
11. These NGOs include the European Women Lobby, European Anti-Poverty Network, International Lesbian and Gay Association (ILGA), European Disability Forum, and Euro Age, among others (Yu 2006: 15).
12. Anti-Discrimination Legislation in EU Member States: A Comparison of National Anti-Discrimination Legislation on the Grounds of Racial or Ethnic Origin, Religion or Belief with the Council Directives. EUMC/MPG, 2002.
13. COM (1999) 564: 8.
14. Black (2000: 16).
15. Staunton (2000: 15).
16. Art. 2(2).
17. Art. 2.2(b).
18. See March 1, 2000, 6435/00, p. 13.
19. See Para. 40, Case C-180/95 *Draehmpaehl* [1997] ECR I-2195.
20. For additional discussion of the negotiations see Chopin (2000); Tyson (2001); Bell (2002); Geddes and Guiraudon (2002).

6

The Politics of Transposition in Britain, France, and Germany*

That [the Anti-Discrimination Law] shall be integrated into the [German Civil Law Code] with its clear systematic liberal approach, one of the masterpieces of European legal culture, has to be regarded as an act of legal vandalism.

Karl-Heinz Ladeur, Dean of the Faculty of Law,
University of Hamburg[1]

6.1 INTRODUCTION

The discourses which drove the passage of the RED did not necessarily translate to the transposition process or the implementation of the laws at the national level. Although the Migration Policy Group and other members of the policy network continued to work at the national and EU level, significant hurdles, both political and in terms of resources, made it difficult to promote the implementation of the RED and equality Directives once they became law, and the transposition process itself faced major hurdles, as we will describe in this chapter. In many cases, the proposed laws faced outright hostility, as seen in the quote at the start of this chapter.

The Racial Equality Directive required the enactment of national legal protections against racial discrimination within three years of its adoption, by July of 2003. As described in the previous chapter, its adoption followed nearly a decade of lobbying by a coalition of NGOs known as the Starting Line Group and was made possible by a propitious set of circumstances that created a window of opportunity for its rapid adoption. Transposition of the RED, however, occurred in different circumstances, and it involved an entirely new and distinct political process, one that in some cases involved domestic actors who were marginalized from the Directive's development and negotiations. Scholars have identified a variety of factors that shape the transposition process. Focusing on events from 2000 to 2007, in this chapter we evaluate the extent to which these factors explain the pattern of transposition observed in Britain, France, and Germany, and we pay particular attention to the role of the MPG and other members of the network in this process. With Britain's long legacy of antidiscrimination legislation, transposition of the RED required relatively minor changes. By contrast, the Directive's provisions did not fit well with German legal traditions, and this fueled arguments against the government's proposals for antidiscrimination legislation. In this chapter, the *timing* and *degree* of national adaptation serve as our dependent variables, and we situate transposition of the RED within the context of political shifts in each country. The following chapter will examine the impact of the European fiscal crisis along with ongoing political issues.

6.2 THE LITERATURE ON TRANSPOSITION

Analysis of the effects of EU policy-making on domestic systems was initially pursued in terms of the degree of *fit* or *misfit* between European rules and domestic institutional and regulatory traditions (Duina 1997, 1999; Knill and Lenschow 1998; Börzel 2000). Where these rules and traditions fit more closely, scholars anticipate that adaptational pressure will be low and that a relatively smooth and unproblematic implementation process will follow. By contrast, greater divergence between national and European rules and traditions is expected to generate higher adaptational pressure that produces contestation, delay, and the possibility of implementation failure. The inadequacies of this structural approach spurred scholars to evaluate the explanatory power of additional variables (Héritier et al. 2001).

New lines of research problematize various "mediating factors" that shape domestic reactions to EU policy imperatives (Risse et al. 2001; Héritier et al. 2001). These factors include the support or opposition of different types of domestic actors, such as political parties and powerful interest groups, as well as the institutional arrangements within which these actors compete for policy-making influence. For example, in her analysis of EU environmental Directives, Tanja Börzel (2000) found that successful transposition depends upon the "pull" pressures exerted by domestic actors, specifically those exerted by supportive environmental groups. Transnational advocacy networks may also act as a mediating factor.

Other scholars, by contrast, emphasize the institutional arrangements within groups competing for policy-making influence. They focus on the number of institutional *veto points*, "stages in the decision-making process on which agreement is legally required for a policy change" (Haverland 2000: 85; Risse et al. 2001; Immergut 1992: 26; Héritier et al. 2001). According to these scholars, a higher number of veto points provides domestic opposition with greater opportunities to modify the transposition outcome (Haverland 2000: 85; Héritier et al. 2001: 5). Thus, the presence of a high number of veto players should stall transposition (Tsebelis 1995, 2002). Indeed, Mark Haverland (2000: 100) found that "veto points tend to shape the timing and quality of implementation regardless of differential gaps in the goodness of fit between European requirements and national traditions." Adrienne Héritier et al. (2001) combine an assessment of fit and misfit with an analysis of the ways in which contending political forces are able to exploit veto points in the policy-making process. They thus "contend that the presence or absence of supportive actor coalitions and veto positions shape a Member State's 'reform capacity.'"

It appears that no single theory explains the transposition of every Directive (Falkner et al. 2007). After evaluating competing theories in the context of a number of Directives across all member states, Gerda Falkner et al. (2007: 403) concluded that "the world seems to be more complicated than both the misfit and the veto player arguments would suggest." A multidimensional approach, therefore, offers the most analytic leverage. In the following section, we generate a number of expectations based upon the degree of policy fit, the availability of veto points, and the presence of supportive or oppositional political actors in each of our three countries.

6.3 EXPECTATIONS

What were the adaptational pressures for Britain, France, and Germany? In order to answer this question, we revisit the main elements of the RED, and we consider key "sticking points" for the three countries that emerged during the RED's negotiations. Based upon these considerations and drawing upon material presented in earlier chapters, our analysis begins by briefly summarizing the degree of policy fit or misfit between the RED and the national settings of Britain, France, and Germany. We do not contend that the so-called "goodness of fit" determines transposition outcomes, but rather we argue that adaptational pressure points give rise to the possibility that domestic actors may interpret their interests in opposition to the Directive and actively seek to thwart its transposition. Domestic veto points condition the likelihood of these actors' success in this regard. National governments confront adaptational pressure points as they translate EU Directives into concrete domestic policy proposals. Political parties thus occupy an important position in shaping the contours of their country's transposition process because their calculations concerning the political environment can shape the nature of the proposals that are submitted for transposition. In addition, the transnational advocacy network may play a role in building a supportive coalition to aid in the transposition process.

For purposes of assessing the degree of policy fit, we focus on five main elements of the RED (see Table 6.1).[2] The first, foundational element of the Directive relates to the acceptance of a race-based discourse that formally recognizes the existence of racial and ethnic differences. Second, the RED defines two types of discrimination (direct and indirect discrimination). A third important element of the RED relates to the scope of the prohibition against discrimination. The Directive's scope encompasses "both the public and private sectors, including public bodies," in relation to a list of specified areas that includes: access to employment; access to vocational training; membership and participation in professional, workers', or employers' organizations; social protection, including social security and healthcare; social advantages; education; and access to goods and services, including housing. Fourth, the RED provides for a shift in the burden of proof so that once a complainant factually establishes that discrimination occurred, the burden shifts to the respondent to prove that it did not. The final key element of the Directive pertains to the issue of enforcement. The RED obliges member states to ensure the availability of judicial or administrative procedures for the enforcement of the Directive's obligations. In addition, it provides that NGOs must be permitted to provide complainants with legal assistance in court, and it requires the creation of an

Table 6.1 Establishing the pre-transposition policy "fit" of the Racial Equality Directive

Key elements of the Racial Equality Directive	Britain	France	Germany
"Race"-based policy discourse	Yes	No	No
Defining discrimination			
Direct discrimination	Yes	No	No
Indirect discrimination	Yes	No	No
Prohibition of discrimination by public entities	Narrower than RED	Yes	Narrower than RED
Prohibition of discrimination by private entities	Yes	Narrower than RED	Narrower than RED
Burden of proof	No	No	No
Type of enforcement procedures	Yes	Criminal only	Limited
Unions & NGOs may provide assistance with legal proceedings to an individual	Yes	Yes	No
Unions & NGOs may engage legal proceedings on behalf of an individual	No	With Restrictions	No
National equality body	Yes	No	No

equality body that is charged with conducting research, making recommendations, and assisting individuals with complaints of discrimination. In analyzing our three cases, we evaluate the extent to which transposition required a *quantitative* (the strengthening or weakening of an existing policy) or *qualitative* (the creation of completely new national institutions or the replacement of existing ones) policy change (Falkner et al. 2005: 27–32).

6.3.1 Britain

As Table 6.1 shows, based upon the "goodness of fit," Britain should present the easiest case for the RED's transposition among the three cases. It alone evidenced a high degree of fit and thus required only quantitative changes that involved strengthening existing policies. Indeed, in some ways, its laws provided broader protection than the RED (EUMC, the United Kingdom, 2002: 19). Its antidiscrimination regime had developed over the preceding 35 years, from the enactment of the Race Relations Act in 1965. As a result, Britain had long accepted a race-based policy discourse, although the precise term used in the RED, "racial origin," was not used in British legislation. Instead, the Race Relations Act of 1976 uses the term "racial grounds," which encompasses color, race, nationality (including citizenship), and ethnic and national origins.[3] The 1976 Act also contains definitions of direct and indirect discrimination, although observers suggested that its definition of indirect discrimination may require modification in order to bring it more closely into line with the RED (EUMC, the United Kingdom, 2002: 10; Cohen 2005).

British law was, however, lacking in two respects. First, with regard to the burden of proof, in the 1990s British courts had set forth conditions under which a court of tribunal could infer that employment discrimination had occurred and look to the employer for an explanation, but this did not constitute a formal shift of the burden of proof.[4] Second, until the law was amended in 2000, the prohibition against racial discrimination was limited in its application to government actions in that it applied only to functions of public authorities that replicated private actions. The requisite adjustments for transposition were thus primarily technical in nature, but not all of them were uncontroversial (Bleich and Feldmann 2004: 23–24).

With regard to enforcement, Britain's pre-RED policies generally complied with the Directive. Its antidiscrimination legislation was enforced solely through the civil courts. It had established an equality body, the Commission on Racial Equality, in 1976. The CRE possessed the power to investigate organizations that it believed were practicing discrimination and issue a binding non-discrimination notice that required an organization to stop discriminating and take action to prevent the discrimination from recurring. It could also issue codes of practice regarding employment and housing, undertake or fund research or educational activities, and with the Secretary of State's approval it could provide funding to organizations concerned with promoting equality of opportunity and good race relations. According to Barbara Cohen (2005: 52), "providing financial support to outside bodies has been a major part of the CRE's functions since it was created." In addition, the CRE was required to consider applications by people seeking legal redress under the Race Relations Act of 1976, and it possessed the power to provide legal assistance, including representation before a court or tribunal. Under the ordinary rules of civil procedure organizations could provide complainants in discrimination cases with legal advice and assistance with case preparation or with financial assistance in order to secure external lawyers' services. Some trade unions and specialized NGOs employ lawyers and therefore can, potentially, offer full support to complainants (Cohen 2005: 47). British antidiscrimination legislation does not, however, permit NGOs or other legal entities, including the CRE, to engage in proceedings on behalf of complainants. In other words, the name of the individual who allegedly experienced the discrimination, as opposed to the organization's name, must be listed as the party initiating the lawsuit.

Despite the close resemblance between preexisting British policy and the RED, two sticking points emerged during the Directive's negotiations. First, British negotiators were very concerned with ensuring that the RED did not apply and could not be extended by means of innovative judicial interpretation to third-country nationals, indicating an ongoing concern with sovereignty over immigration policy. Second, they were concerned over the definition of indirect discrimination.

In terms of the "mediating factors" that may also shape transposition, Britain seemed to be in a strong position for relatively quick and comprehensive compliance. The requisite law reforms seemingly enjoyed the support of powerful domestic actors. Most importantly, New Labour governed Britain during the entire period of transposition. Because Labour governments had constructed Britain's antidiscrimination policy regime and because Labour was more favorably predisposed to the EU, at least on this particular policy issue, this fact would seem to auger well for a smooth, thorough, and easy transposition process. In addition, as a legacy of Britain's longstanding antidiscrimination regime, antidiscrimination policy enjoyed a large preexisting constituency among activists and lawyers that could lobby in support of the RED's transposition. A lack of significant veto points in the British legislative process constitutes a final factor that would seem to facilitate the RED's easy transposition. Britain transposed the RED through two measures—the Race Relations (Amendment) Act 2000, the genesis of which predated the formal transposition period, and the Race Relations Act 1976 (Amendment) Regulations 2003, which served as the formal vehicle for transposing the RED.

6.3.2 France

Based upon the level of policy fit, we would expect France to experience greater difficulty than Britain in transposing the RED (see Table 6.1). The Directive's transposition would require a significant qualitative shift in important elements of French law and policy. France had developed a domestic policy regime against racism that differed in important ways from that of the RED (Bleich 2003: chapters 6–7). It had historically resisted calls to distinguish among its citizens on the basis of race or origin. As discussed in Chapter 5 French discomfort with the very idea of *race* manifested itself during the negotiations. Rather than prohibit racial discrimination, French law prohibited expressions of racial hatred and violence. Thus, it would need to enact definitions of discrimination into law. During the RED's negotiations, France expressed resistance to accepting a definition of indirect discrimination that would require the collection of statistical data on racial or ethnic groups. The collection of such data was prohibited by law in France.

France first made racial discrimination illegal with Law No. 72-546 of July 1, 1972. This law criminalized the refusal, or conditional offer, to provide goods or services as well as the decision not to employ or dismiss an individual on grounds of race, religion, ethnicity, or national origin. Five years later, Law No. 77-574 of June 7, 1977 expanded the scope of this prohibition to include interference in the exercise of economic activity. Finally, a Law of July 22, 1992 precluded reliance upon a "legitimate motive" as a justification for discrimination, and it increased the penalties. In addition, the Labor Code contains a number of provisions that in many instances duplicate provisions of the foregoing penal laws (Recht 2002: 13–14).

In addition, judicial traditions and procedures concerning France's criminal and civil legal systems complicate national compliance with the RED. French anti-racism laws were enforced primarily by penal sanctions, which actually facilitated a complainant's access to evidence that was in the defendant's possession because in criminal matters judges possess broad inquisitorial powers. This is especially important in France where copying an employer's documents is regarded as theft (Latraverse 2007). Under the rules of civil procedure, by contrast, access to such evidence is made very difficult because in civil matters the judge does not perform an inquisitorial role (Latraverse 2007). Thus, the French legal system does not fit well with the working assumptions that underlie the RED.

Despite the benefits of France's criminal approach, there existed problems with the laws' enforcement. Mouloud Aounit, Secretary-General of the Movement against Racism and for Friendship among Peoples (MRAP), reportedly described the French law as "an empty shell, unenforced and inefficient" (Marlowe 2001: 6). Moreover, despite widespread racial discrimination in employment, "only four French employers were convicted in 1999" (Marlowe 2001: 6). France also did not have a national equality body, although in 1999, it established the Group to Study and Combat Discrimination (GELD).[5] GELD, however, had little more than research and promotional functions, and it did little beyond managing a hotline for reporting discrimination that was created in 2001.

In terms of "mediating factors" that may also shape transposition, France appeared to occupy a weaker position than that of Britain. Like Britain, it too was governed by a social democratic party, the *Parti Socialiste* (PS), but only through late April 2002, at which time Lionel Jospin lost in the first round of the presidential election and announced his political retirement. This offered a narrow window of political opportunity for the enactment of national legislation. Moreover, France lacked a strong domestic constituency committed to lobbying on behalf of the RED's transposition. Its anti-racism NGOs historically did not see litigation as a tool for advancing their interests, even though the law accorded them a role in the enforcement (Sophie Latraverse, personal interview, June 3, 2004), and French pro-migrant organizations had shown little interest in EU developments (Geddes and Guiraudon 2004: 341). In fact, the only experts on antidiscrimination law in France were women who developed their expertise as a result of the transposition of EU Directives concerning sex discrimination into French law. Similar to the British, the French system has relatively few veto points. Although the RED was initially transposed during a time of cohabitation, with President Chirac coming from a right party and Prime Minister Jospin coming from the left, there was little disagreement over the RED, given the need for both parties to respond to the radical right.

France transposed the RED in two main steps. The Jospin government transposed most of the Directive's key elements into French law through two measures: Law No. 1006-2001 of November 16, 2001 and the law of social modernization No. 2002-73 of January 17, 2002. The creation of a national equality body remained the only major element of the RED that had been left unfulfilled at the end of the Jospin government. The conservative government of Jacques Chirac completed the transposition process with Law No. 2004-1486 of December 30, 2004 that created a national equality body, the High Authority against Discrimination and for Equality (HALDE). Given the low degree of policy fit and the weakness of any domestic constituency in support of the RED, what explains the Directive's quick and relatively comprehensive transposition?

6.3.3 Germany

Finally, relative to both Britain and France, Germany presented a total misfit in terms of its preexisting law and policies (Won-Pil Suh and Bales 2006: 291). Its Constitution, the Basic Law, prohibited discrimination by the state on a number of grounds, including race, but Germany lacked a dedicated antidiscrimination law. Although it had a variety of labor laws that contained provisions concerning equal treatment, these laws were premised upon a "concept of employer responsibility," rather than on a concept of civil rights" (Baer 2005: 5). Moreover, "under German law, the prevailing principles are those of freedom of contract and the employer's discretionary power to select employees" (Won-Pil Suh and Bales 2006: 291). As a result, at the turn of the twenty-first century, antidiscrimination legislation was not seen as a "field of law in its own right" (Baer 2005: 5). Transposition of the RED would thus require significant qualitative reforms.

Germany's preexisting laws concerning racism and discrimination consisted of criminal sanctions against racism and anti-Semitism. These laws originated as part of the country's reaction to the Holocaust. Germany had not adopted a race-based policy discourse like that of Britain in large part because it still regarded its minority population as "temporary" and because many members of its minority communities did not possess German citizenship, despite having been born and raised in Germany. During the negotiations, Germany expressed discomfort with the RED's broad application to what it regarded as "private" transactions between non-state actors. Indeed, as we showed in Chapter 5 it managed to secure modified language and a recital that would provide it with greater flexibility in transposing the RED.

Yet, the German political environment provided a mixed picture for transposition. The German system contains important veto points. Peter Katzenstein (1987), for example, emphasizes the decentralized nature of the German state and the highly centralized and powerful societal interests, most notably employers' organizations and trade unions. The *Bundesrat* (upper chamber) checks the federal government's power with its ability to veto legislation (Tsebelis 1995). Its veto threat has grown in recent years due to developments in party politics at the state level that make it much more difficult for the parties in federal government to attain and maintain the absolute majority of votes in the *Bundesrat* (König and Bräuninger 1997).

Since 1998, Gerhard Schröder had governed with a coalition of the SPD and the Greens (*Grüne*). It was the country's first government since 1920 to contain no right-of-center parties and the first government in which the Greens participated at the national level (Pulzer 2003: 153). However, Germany did not transpose the RED until August 2006, one year after an election that replaced Schröder's SPD–Greens government with a grand coalition led by Angela Merkel of the Christian Democratic Union (*Christlich Demokratische Union Deutschlands*, CDU)—an event that observers predicted would trigger "the slow death of far-reaching anti-discrimination legislation" (Clüver 2004). Our analysis emphasizes the SPD's tepid support for antidiscrimination legislation, combined with a mobilized opposition and the availability of critical veto points in the German political system.

6.3.4 The Transnational Advocacy Network

Although the SLG dissolved after achieving its goal vis-à-vis the RED, key figures from the SLG continued to cooperate through new networking structures, particularly the European Network against Racism (ENAR) and the Migration Policy Group, headed by the SLG's leader, Jan Niessen. Additional opportunities for influence became available through the European Commission's European Community Action Programme to Combat Discrimination (2001–2006) that was established in order to support the effective implementation of the new antidiscrimination Directives. For example, in 2000, at the European Commission's request, the MPG and the Netherlands-based "Human European Consultancy" (another think tank) established the European Network of Legal Experts in the non-discrimination field. This Network is charged with providing the Commission with independent information and advice on the implementation and application of the Article 13 antidiscrimination Directives.[6] These new institutions and programs, among others, enabled the transnational advocacy network to monitor the national transposition of the RED.

For example, the European Network of Legal Experts prepared annual reports on each member state's transposition effort, and these reports were made available on the websites of the MPG and the European Commission. In 2002, the EUMC published a series of reports that compared existing antidiscrimination legislation in EU member states with the RED. The information upon which these reports were based was provided by a group of independent experts pursuant to a joint initiative of the MPG, Interights, and the European Roma Rights Centre (ERRC) entitled *Implementing European Anti-Discrimination Law*.[7] Draft reports for this project were prepared in time for submission to the Legal Working Group that was convened by the European Commission in November 2001 for purposes of preparing for the Directives' transposition into national law. From 2002, the MPG managed the European Network of Equality Bodies (Equinet). Finally, a vast number of reports were published, reporting on transposition efforts and implementing the RED (Chopin 2000; EUMC/MPG 2000; ERRC/Interights/MPG 2001; Niessen and Chopin 2004; Chopin et al. 2004). The network's influence can be at least partially assessed by determining the extent to which these actors met their goals during the transposition process and the hurdles they faced with the politics which would ultimately play a role in implementation.

6.4 THE POLITICS OF TRANSPOSITION IN BRITAIN

The issue of race was highly visible in Britain at the time of the RED's adoption. In the late 1990s, domestic developments had been independently driving Britain toward further reform of its antidiscrimination laws, reform that would facilitate greater national compliance with the new Directive's terms. The 1993 murder in southeast London of Stephen Lawrence provided the impetus for this reform effort. The police bungled the investigation, and as a result, the main suspects in the case were not convicted. The case generated high levels of media attention and elevated the issue of racism on the public agenda (Cottle 2005). Others have detailed the events surrounding the murder and its investigation (e.g., Hall 1999; BBC 1999; Cottle 2004). For our purposes, the significance of these events lies in the policy shift that followed. New Labour came to power in 1997, and it commissioned an inquiry into Stephen Lawrence's murder and the subsequent police investigation. In February 1999, this inquiry released its report, commonly known as the "McPherson Report" after its chair Sir William McPherson.[8] The report highlighted the existence of "institutional racism" in Britain, and it recommended that *all* functions of public bodies be brought within the scope of the Race Relations Act of 1976.

In response to the McPherson Report, the Blair government introduced into Parliament the Race Relations (Amendment) Bill, a measure that would extend coverage of the 1976 Act to police and other public officials that were previously exempt from the law against racial discrimination under the so-called "public authorities" exception (Guild 2000: 417) and obligate public sector institutions to promote equal treatment. The EU thus adopted the RED just as Britain was considering its own legislation that would significantly reform the country's antidiscrimination policy regime in ways that would satisfy the Directive's requirements. The Race Relations (Amendment) Act 2000 received royal assent on November 30, 2000. It extended the Race Relations Act's scope to nearly all functions of public authorities, thus satisfying one of the RED's main requirements.

However, reflecting Britain's concerns with the intersection of antidiscrimination law and immigration, this legislation contained two special exceptions. First, although it brought within the scope of the Race Relations Act 1976 *all* functions of public authorities, one provision of the Act allows a minister to authorize discrimination on grounds of nationality and ethnic or national origins in executing specified immigration control functions.[9] In April 2001, Home Office Minister Barbara Roche signed such an authorization that empowered immigration officers to refuse entry to individuals belonging to seven ethnic or national groups strictly on the basis of their race or nationality.[10] Second, the Labour government strengthened the exception that permits discrimination based upon a person's place of ordinary residence or the length of time that a person has been in Britain if this action is taken pursuant to statutory authority or any arrangements made or approved by a Minister of the Crown (Cohen 2005: 35).

Because the Race Relations (Amendment) Act 2000 did not transpose the RED completely, in 2001 the Blair government began work on completing the transposition process. It provided multiple opportunities for members of the transnational advocacy network to try to influence the process. The

Home Office served as lead government department concerned with implementing the RED. The consultation process began in 2002 with the publication of *Towards Equality and Diversity*, which set forth the government's general approach and explained the RED's main features in simple language. Individuals and organizations responded with over 850 submissions. The government released two subsequent consultation documents. *Equality and Diversity—The Way Ahead* was published in October 2002 and set out the government's specific proposals for new regulations, and *Equality and Diversity— Making it Happen* solicited views on the arrangements and institutions that would best suit the legislation. In addition, it convened a series of events around the country, including roundtable discussions between ministers and NGO representatives. Over 4,000 responses were received through various consultations (European Commission 2004: 9). A large number of NGOs had sprung up around Britain's longstanding antidiscrimination laws. Many of these organizations were members of the TAN, most notably the CRE. For example, the CRE served as the EUMC's "National Focal Point," and in this capacity, it prepared reports on discrimination in employment, education, and housing as well as Britain's new implementing legislation.[11]

The government chose to transpose the RED by means of regulations introduced under the European Communities Act (1972) rather than through primary legislation.[12] The European Communities Act 1972 provides for a relatively easy and efficient procedure through which EU legislation can be transposed into British law. However, this procedure limits the scope of the regulations to that of the Directive, and it has important consequences where preexisting legislation on the same matter is broader than that of the Directive, as was the case with regard to Britain's race relations legislation (Cohen 2005: 2; Geddes and Guiraudon 2007: 138). Recall that the Race Relations Act 1976 protects against discrimination on a wider array of grounds that includes color, nationality (including citizenship), and national origin as well as racial grounds and ethnic origin, whereas the RED applies only to racial and ethnic origin. As a result of using this method of transposition, the resultant law is riddled with "anomalies and inconsistencies" (Cohen 2005: 2). Specifically, the Race Relations Act 1976 (Amendment) Regulations 2003 creates a "two-track structure" in which different definitions of indirect discrimination and different rules on the burden of proof apply (Cohen 2005: 2, 56).[13] The new, wider definition of indirect discrimination and the shift in the burden of proof applies where the alleged discrimination occurs on grounds of race or ethnic origins and in relation to the scope of activities provided for in the RED.[14] The original definition of indirect discrimination under the Race Relations Act 1976, by contrast, continues to apply where the grounds of alleged discrimination are those of color or nationality and in areas not covered by the RED. Likewise, the law does not provide for a shift in the burden of proof on these grounds and in these areas.

In 2006, the Labour government amalgamated the three specialty equality bodies—the CRE, the Equal Opportunities Commission, which focused on gender equality, and the Disability Rights Commission—into the Equality and Human Rights Commission (EHRC).[15] This new body continues the work of its three predecessors. In addition, the EHRC promotes equality with regard to age, sexual orientation, and religion or belief, and the protection of human rights. The Commission possesses similar enforcement powers to those of the CRE with regard to combating racial and ethnic discrimination.

6.5 THE POLITICS OF TRANSPOSITION IN FRANCE

The Jospin government got off to a quick start in transposing the RED, enacting two laws before its collapse in June 2002. Following 13 months of discussion, on November 16, 2001 the National Assembly passed a bill on combating employment discrimination (Law No. 1006-2001) that had been sponsored by Jean Le Garrec, the Socialist chair of the National Assembly's Social Affairs Committee. On January 7, 2002 it enacted the Law of Social Modernization No. 2002-73. Together, these measures implement important elements of the RED. They provide for the requisite shift in the burden of proof in all non-criminal cases, except in those that involve claims of employment discrimination by employees of the public sector. In these cases, existing law provides for an inquisitorial, administrative procedure in which the complainant does not bear the burden of proof. However, there are shortcomings. Although the new laws speak of direct and indirect discrimination, they do not provide definitions of these terms (Latraverse 2007).

With regard to enforcement, these laws reshaped enforcement mechanisms in several important ways. They give trade unions a right to pursue antidiscrimination claims in the courts on behalf of employees who claim to have suffered racial discrimination. Unions may do so without the alleged victim's written consent so long as they have provided the individual with written notification of their intention and they have not received a notice of opposition from the individual within a 15-day period. The law also authorizes NGOs that have been working in the antidiscrimination area for at least five years to act in court on behalf of alleged victims of racial discrimination so long as they obtain the individual's written consent.

The creation of an independent equality body proved more difficult, but political developments in 2002 created a more favorable environment for this reform. Creation of an independent body authorized to investigate complaints of racial discrimination in employment had been recommended in an April 1999 report by the High Council on Integration, an advisory body that had been established in 1989.[16] By the late 1990s, elements of the French right were beginning to appreciate the political mileage that may lie in antidiscrimination policy. For example, Alain Juppé, leader of the conservative Rally for the Republic, acknowledged the problem of discrimination and realized the potential value of attracting immigrant voters (Geddes and Guiraudon 2002; Guiraudon 2004). According to Andrew Geddes and Virginie Giraudon (2002: 26), he "realized that as populations of migrant origin became more diversified socially, they were likely to be more politically diverse as well and not only left-leaning as when they were comprised of factory workers." The FN's Jean-Marie Le Pen received the second-highest proportion of the vote (16.86 percent) in the first round of the 2002 presidential election. Although Le Pen lost decisively to Jacques Chirac (*Union pour un Mouvement Populaire*, UMP) in the run-off election that followed two weeks later, his electoral performance nevertheless generated national embarrassment and made it imperative for the subsequent conservative government to distance itself from the racist radical right through further action on antidiscrimination policy. As a result, President Chirac quickly promised that his government would establish a national equality body in order to combat the rise of racist and anti-Semitic behavior in France.

President Chirac charged Bernard Stasi, Ombudsman of the French Republic, with the task of defining a potential framework for establishing a national equality body. Over 100 hearings were scheduled between July 10 and December 17, 2003. They involved public services and ministries, voluntary sector organizations, trade unions, political parties, and experts. In 2004, the French government announced its plan, one that appeared to draw inspiration from the British and Belgian models (Kretzschmar et al. 2004: 1). With Act No. 2004-1486, France established the HALDE on December 30, 2004. This law gave HALDE the authority to investigate all forms of discrimination that are prohibited by law or are contrary to an international convention ratified by France. Individuals as well as NGOs and national and European MEPs may file written claims with HALDE. In the course of its investigations, HALDE can request explanations from any private or public body and order the submission of documents. Individuals who fail to comply with HALDE's requests can be compelled to comply by court order. Table 6.2 outlines key events in the transposition of the RED in France.

The Chirac government expanded HALDE's powers in 2006 as part of its reaction to urban rioting. In October 2005, two French youths of Malian and Tunisian descent were electrocuted as they hid from police in an electrical substation in the Parisian suburb of Clichy-sous-Bois. Nearly three weeks of rioting followed throughout the Paris region and several major French cities. At a press conference on December 1, 2005, the Prime Minister declared equal opportunities to be a "major national cause for 2006." In addition, President Chirac admitted that France suffered from the "'poison of discrimination,'"

Table 6.2 Timeline of major transposition developments in France

Law	Date	Party in power	Significance
Law No. 1006-2001	November 16, 2001	*Parti Socialiste*	Prohibits discrimination in employment
Law of Social Modernization No. 2002-73	January 7, 2002	*Parti Socialiste*	Prohibits discrimination in access to housing on grounds of nationality, physical appearance, political belief, health, ethnic origin, trade union activity, religion, disability, age, or sexual orientation
Law No. 2004-1486	December 30, 2004	*Union pour un Mouvement Populaire*	Established the High Authority against Discrimination and for Equality (HALDE)
Equal Opportunity Act No. 2006-396	March 31, 2006	*Union pour un Mouvement Populaire*	Authorized HALDE to make settlement agreements

and Interior Minister Nicolas Sarkozy deplored 30 years of failed French policies that had left the children of immigrants without hope (Button 2005). On
February 1, 2006, the government announced an action plan.

On January 11, 2006, the government presented to the National Assembly
an Equal Opportunities Bill that was ultimately enacted three months later.[17]
This legislation was prepared by Azouz Begag, the minister with responsibility
for the Promotion of Equal Opportunities, and Jean-Louis Borloo, Minister
for Employment, Social Cohesion and Housing (French Ministry of Foreign
Affairs 2006a: 3). It contains important provisions that strengthened enforcement capacity. It provides a legal basis for "situation testing" under French
criminal law. This would allow organizations to use a tactic to gather evidence
of discrimination that has been long used in the U.S. and Britain. Essentially,
individuals of different races are sent to apply for a job or housing, etc., in
order to determine whether discrimination is occurring. In addition, the
Equal Opportunities Act authorized HALDE to conduct situation testing. In
conjunction with this legislation, the Ministry of Justice issued a ministerial
instruction to public prosecutors and the president of each court of appeal that
provided guidelines for the new law's enforcement, particularly concerning
the rules of evidence (Rorive 2009: 64–65).[18] Finally, the Equal Opportunities
Act also strengthened HALDE's powers by giving it authority to make settle-
ment agreements that—upon approval by the Public Prosecutor—may result
in fines (French Ministry of Foreign Affairs 2006b).

In the French case, the ongoing influence of the radical right and domestic unrest influenced the quick passage of legislation that implemented most of the RED's main terms and continued to influence the strengthening of this legislation. In addition, French NGOs developed closer ties with the transnational advocacy network. Two organizations served as national contacts, "National Focal Points," within the EUMC's network. There were the Centre d'Etudes des Discriminations, du Racisme et de l'Antisémitisme (CEDRA) and the *Agence pour le développement des relations interculturelles* (Agency for the Development of Intercultural Relations, ADRI) that became the EUMC's "National Focal Point" for France, and in this capacity wrote a series of reports on employment discrimination among minorities and migrants in France, discrimination in education and housing, and a report on France's implementing legislation.[19]

6.6 THE POLITICS OF TRANSPOSITION IN GERMANY

Despite a low degree of policy fit between the RED and Germany's domestic laws and policies, between 2000 and 2003 transposition of the Directive appeared to be politically possible. Gerhard Schröder's Social Democrats had governed since 1998 in coalition with the Greens. Yet, multiple efforts by the SPD–Greens government to transpose the RED through legislation failed. An initial 2001 proposal was never introduced into Parliament, and two subsequent bills, one in 2002 and another in 2005, lapsed with the prorogation of Parliament for elections. It took six years, the initiation of infringement proceedings in the ECJ,[20] and paradoxically, the election of a conservative-led "grand coalition" before compliant antidiscrimination legislation was finally enacted. Its delayed transposition of the RED was caused by the absence of strong support for the legislation, the presence of strong opposition, and the ability of this opposition to exploit veto points in the German political system. In contrast to France, which also faced a degree of policy misfit, German politicians did not face a threat from the radical right. This, we suggest, enabled them to play a different kind of politics.

Table 6.3 sets forth the sequence of proposals that occurred during Germany's transposition process that lasted from 2000 through August 2006. It shows that the Schröder government made three unsuccessful attempts to enact antidiscrimination legislation. These proposals are notable because of their breadth. The 2001 proposal would have amended the Civil Law Code to prohibit discrimination on all of the grounds specified in Article 13 of the Treaty of Amsterdam. However, it would have excluded the area of employment, a policy area that was not within the Ministry's competency. The Ministry of

Table 6.3 Timeline of major transposition developments in Germany

Legislative proposal	Date	Parties in power	Significance	Outcome
Discussion Draft Law on the Prevention of Discrimination in the Private Sector (Ministry of Justice)	Issued December 10, 2001	SPD–Greens	Prohibited discrimination on all Article 13 grounds in general contract law, access to occupational associations; did not apply to employment and did not provide for the creation of a national equality body	Abandoned in April 2002 before the election campaign; never introduced into the *Bundestag*
Ministry of Justice released a revised Discussion Draft	February 17, 2002			Never introduced into the *Bundestag*
Draft of a Law for the conversion of European Antidiscrimination Guidelines (*Antidiskriminierungsgesetz*, ADG)	December 16, 2004	SPD–Greens	Prohibited discrimination on grounds of race, ethnicity, gender, religion or belief, disability, age or sexual identity in general contract law, public and private employment; provided for the creation of a national equality body; provided for shift in the burden of proof; it covered 2000/43/EC, 2000/78/EC, 2000/73/EC and 2004/113/EC	Approved by the *Bundestag* in June 2005; rejected by the *Bundesrat* in July 2005; a *Bundesrat* mediation committee could not negotiate a compromise
	January 2006			Same draft legislation was again introduced into the parliament (Lower house, *Bundestag*) and dropped
General Equal Treatment Act (*Allgemeines Gleichbehandlungsgesetz*, AGG[a])	2006	CDU–SPD	Prohibits discrimination on grounds of gender, race, ethnic background, and sexual orientation or religion in employment and created the *Die Antidiskriminierungsstelle des Bundes* (Federal Antidiscrimination Office)	Entered into force August 18, 2006

[a] Available at <http://www.gesetze-im-internet.de/agg/BJNR189710006.html>.

Justice promised that a separate regulation addressing employment would be offered later. They included all of the Article 13 grounds, namely race and ethnic origin, that appear in the RED, and religion or belief, age, disability, gender, and sexual orientation that appear in the Employment Equality Directive (Directive 2000/78, November 27, 2000).

The Red–Green coalition was ineffective in transposing the RED for four main reasons. First, transposition was undermined by the timing of the government's effort—it did not attempt to enact antidiscrimination legislation until after it had reformed Germany's citizenship laws. Second, the two coalition partners were not equally committed to antidiscrimination legislation. The Greens sought a broad measure that transposed both the RED and the Employment Equality Directive, whereas the SPD was far less enthusiastic. Third, the breadth of the government's proposals in conjunction with the novelty of antidiscrimination legislation in Germany mobilized a highly vocal and powerful set of opposition forces within civil society. The domestic coalition that supported the idea of antidiscrimination was relatively weaker, and as further evidence of the poor fit, it, too, had difficulties with the idea of racial antidiscrimination legislation. Finally, these opposition forces were able to exploit the *Bundesrat,* a key veto point in the German political system, to stall the government's legislation. We examine each of these reasons in greater detail.

First, antidiscrimination legislation was undermined by the sequence in which the government pursued its citizenship and antidiscrimination reforms. Reform of Germany's citizenship laws was a higher political priority for the Greens and the SPD, and the government pursued this controversial policy area first. Declaring that Germany is "a country of immigrants," its proposal represented a dramatic departure from Germany's existing laws in two ways. First, it essentially proposed abolishing the *jus sanguinis* principle by giving German citizenship to children born in Germany to non-German parents, and second, it proposed officially accepting for the first time the concept of dual-citizenship. The Christian Democrats (CDU), with the support of the Free Democrats (*Freie Demokratische Partei,* FDP), postured themselves conservatively on the issue by introducing a proposal into the *Bundesrat* that would have restricted the country's immigration intake. At the time, a poll released by the newspaper *Die Woche* found that 75 percent of respondents supported a reduction in the country's immigration intake, despite reports that Germany would require 400,000 immigrants a year in order to sustain its social welfare state.[21] The conservative parties sought to politicize the issue of immigration for purposes of the impending election in the state of Hesse, set for February 7, 1999 (Amiya-Nakada 2007: 7). Although opinion polls in Hesse had been predicting the election of a Red–Green coalition, the Christian Democrats won 43.4 percent of the vote and formed a coalition government with the FDP. The Schröder government consequently lost its majority in the *Bundesrat* after a mere four months in power. In order to transpose the RED through legislation, it would thereafter be required to obtain the approval of the opposition parties at the federal level. A modified version of the government's citizenship law was ultimately enacted in May 1999 after the government struck a deal with the FDP, but by then the political damage had been done.[22]

Second, from the outset, the SPD and the Greens were not equally committed to antidiscrimination legislation. In contrast to the Greens, whose platform advocated the adoption of antidiscrimination legislation that would protect various minorities, including racial and ethnic minorities, the SPD's platform was limited to antidiscrimination measures concerning gender. The 1998 coalition agreement, however, reflected the Green Party's influence. It contained a commitment to enact legislation that would prohibit discrimination and encourage equal treatment. Yet, the post of Minister of Justice was given to Social Democrat Herta Däubler-Gmelin, a member of the less sympathetic coalition partner. It was not until December 10, 2001, halfway through the RED's three-year transposition period, that the Ministry of Justice released its first proposal for an antidiscrimination law. This measure, however, lapsed with the calling of a new election in September 2002, at which the Red–Green coalition was returned to power. This is not to say, however, that the Red–Green government was not interested in fighting right-wing extremism; in fact, it gave a great deal of financial support to civil society for such programs (Hieronymus and Moses 2002: 4).

This same disparate commitment characterized the parties' 2002 election platforms (see Bündnis 90/Die Grünen 2002). Following the government's reelection, the new coalition agreement preserved the commitment to transposing the RED through new legislation. Again, however, the SPD named the Minister of Justice. This time it chose Brigitte Zypries, who was even more hostile to the antidiscrimination law than was her predecessor. In March 2003, the *Frankfurter Alljemeine Zeitang* (*FAZ*) newspaper reported that Zypries did not fully support antidiscrimination legislation (Amiya-Nakada 2007: 11; *FAZ*, March 7, 2003). Zypries reportedly stated that Germany's "'Civil Code is the land of private autonomy'" and that "'civic freedoms in the liberal state includes…making distinctions and treating unequally'" on official occasions (Amiya-Nakada 2007: 11; see also Zypries 2003a, 2003b, 2004). Moreover, in 2003 Chancellor Schröder publicly stated that he wanted to avoid the creation of a "'bureaucratic monster'" that could be regarded as a new hindrance by business (quoted in Funk 2003). As the government's second proposal was being debated by Parliament in 2005, the Greens convened an expert conference, entitled "Tailwind from Europe," on the need for legislation to transpose the EU Directives (Amiya-Nakada 2007: 11). Meanwhile, however, key political figures in the SPD government of Germany's largest state and one-time SPD stronghold, North Rhine Westphalia, harshly criticized the antidiscrimination bill in the lead-up to the May 2005 *Landtag* election and threatened not to support it in the *Bundesrat* (Amiya-Nakada 2007: 12).

Third, a vocal and powerful opposition mobilized in response to the government's proposed antidiscrimination legislation. Critics of the antidiscrimination bills advanced three main claims. First, they argued that they were redundant. Second, they claimed that discrimination was not a problem in Germany. Third, they asserted that enactment of such laws would have severe detrimental consequences for the German economy and society. Employers' organizations opposed the legislation, portraying it as a threat to the German economy. For example, Dieter Hundt, President of the Confederation of German Employers' Associations (*Bundesvereinigung der deutschen Arbeitgeberverbände*, BDA) asserted that the proposed law was the product of "'unrealistic, missionary and ideological bureaucrats'" and promised "'a lot of new red tape and dynamite for the German economic order'" (quoted in Funk 2003). In addition, during debate on the government's 2004 proposal, the Federal Association of Employers convened a symposium entitled "Secure the freedom of contract!" (Amiya-Nakada 2007: 11).

The legal community was also hostile. For example, law professor Karl-Heinz Ladeur (2002) characterized the 2002 proposal "an act of legal vandalism." Lawyers specifically criticized the shifting of the burden of proof, the intervention of organizations in legal actions, and "state intervention in the sphere of the Civil Code itself" (Amiya-Nakada 2007: 9). In addition, inclusion of religion as a prohibited ground of discrimination fueled opposition from the Catholic and Protestant Churches. Religious leaders feared a loss of exemptions that, for example, allowed them to require teachers in church-operated schools to be members of the faith and to give preference to children of its particular religion in the admissions process (Won-Pil Suh and Bales 2006).

A number of powerful interests organized in opposition to the Directives' transposition, including employers' organizations, business interests, churches, and important elements of the legal community. This is not to say, however, that the idea of antidiscrimination legislation was without support. Within Germany, a number of critiques had emerged concerning the absence of antidiscrimination legislation (Aukerman 1995; Wilpert 2003). Trade unions had supported antidiscrimination legislation. For example, in 1990, the union of civil servants published a draft antidiscrimination law (Hammer and Rzadkowski 1991: 363). The Federation of German Trade Unions (*Deutscher Gewerkschaftsbund*, DGB) supported the government's proposed laws (Funk 2003). Nevertheless, scholars agree that relatively few organized groups lobbied on behalf of the laws' antiracism element (Bleich and Feldmann 2004: 23) and that German pro-migrant organizations had shown little interest in EU developments (Geddes and Guiraudon 2004: 341).

Working through ENAR, German NGOs waged an information campaign that sought to document the problems faced by minorities in Germany. Writing in 2002, Hieronymus and Moses (2002: 24) observed in the Shadow Report that "knowledge about acts of discrimination is poor in Germany." The European Forum for Migration Studies (EFMS) Institute at the University of Bamberg served as Germany's "National Focal Point" within the EUMC network, and in this capacity wrote a series of reports on discrimination against minorities and migrants in employment, education, and housing as well as a report on the state of antidiscrimination law in Germany.[23] In 2002, ENAR released a "Shadow Report" entitled *Talking "Race" in Germany* that was funded by the European Commission and produced by Dr. Andreas Hieronymus and Meena Moses, iMiR—*Institut für Migrations- und Rassismusforschung* (Institute for Migration and Race Studies), an ENAR member. It described the problems of racism and discrimination in Germany. This is important because few studies of discrimination in Germany existed at the time (Hieronymus and Moses 2002: 22). In December 2001, the League against Ethnic Discrimination in the Federal Republic of Germany (*Bund gegen ethnische Diskriminierung in der Bundesrepublik Deutschland*, BDB) published a report about five years of experience in working in the field of antidiscrimination in Berlin and Brandenburg.

Groups that were in favor of the RED were dissatisfied with the December 2001 proposal. For example, in February 2002, PRO ASLY, a pro-asylum seeker organization that was also a member of ENAR, released a statement that criticized the bill's narrow scope for not fully implementing the RED.[24] This same month, a set of ten organizations from the state of North-Rhine Westphalia released a critical position paper, observing that the proposal was far less than that adopted in other EU member states and noting that a good law would be a signal of great importance, since racism was once national policy in Germany.[25] They called for the inclusion of administration, police, and the judiciary in the law and banning all forms of institutional discrimination occurring because of the "Alien Laws" (*Ausländergesetze*).

Part of the difficulty in mobilizing a supportive domestic constituency lay in a profound discursive misfit. Translating the term *race* from international documents into German as *Rasse* is "problematic" because in Germany the concepts of "race" and "ethnicity" are generally perceived as "essentialist" categories that represent the "'Wesen' (essence) of a 'Volk' (tribe) in academic and popular discourse" (Hieronymus and Moses 2002: 4). Moreover, because "the concept of racism carries the stigma of colonialism and the Holocaust," Andreas Hieronymus and Meena Moses (2002: 4) observe that it is "rather difficult to talk about 'race' in German." In fact, this was one reason why Hieronymus and Moses wrote their 2002 Shadow Report in English. Some NGOs criticized the 2001 bill's use of the term *Rasse*. For example, the group *Netz gegen Rassismus* (Net against Racism, NgR), which was formally linked to ENAR, released critiques of the government's 2001 and 2006 proposals. In these, it expressed its desire to have the term *Rasse* deleted from the bills, and it wanted nationality included instead.[26]

Difficulty also arose due to the legislation's poor institutional fit with civil society. Many of these organizations were concerned more broadly with issues concerning citizenship, immigration, and asylum policies. Further, as Hieronymus and Moses (2002: 23) observe:

> Many organizations involved in counseling migrants do good social work, but they do not explicitly tackle the issues of discrimination. While the headquarters of such large organizations (often linked to churches or trade unions) insist that they have worked in the field of anti-discrimination for a long time, it shows that on a local level, it is very difficult, because there is little awareness about racist discrimination and the perspectives of victims.

Further, in 2002, Germany lacked a "nationwide structure for operating antidiscrimination offices," with the exception of the states of North Rhine-Westphalia, Berlin, and Brandenburg where grassroots organizations were trying to create such an infrastructure and develop an information base that documents the problem of discrimination (Hieronymus and Moses 2002: 23). According to the Antiracist Information Centre (ARIC), which operates in North Rhine-Westphalia and Berlin, there exists little political support for this kind of infrastructure (Hieronymus and Moses 2002: 23).

After the SPD lost the May 2005 *Landtag* election in North Rhine-Westphalia, Chancellor Schröder purposely lost a vote of confidence in the *Bundestag* on July 1, and three weeks later President Horst Köhler dissolved the chamber, paving the way for an early election on September 18, 2005. According to Cathryn Clüver (2004), antidiscrimination legislation was "the 'hot-button' topic" in the lead-up to the election in North Rhine-Westphalia, and during this period Angela Merkel "announced that reversing the outgoing Social Democrat Government's course with respect to anti-discrimination legislation would be one of her first missions in office if she was elected as chancellor." The CDU maintained that the passage of antidiscrimination legislation was unnecessary because the Basic Law already provided for equality (Clüver 2004). Unsurprisingly, efforts by the conciliatory committee that arbitrates between the federal government and the *Bundesrat* (the *Vermittlungsausschuss*) to negotiate a compromise on an antidiscrimination law failed, and the country went to elections without having transposed the RED. Ultimately, however, as Chancellor, Merkel oversaw the enactment of the General Equal Treatment Act (*Allgemeines Gleichbehandlungsgesetz*, AGG). Germany's compliance was driven by the fact that the ECJ had launched infringement proceedings against Germany and issued a fine against the country.[27] On July 29, 2004, one year after transposition was to have occurred, the Commission initiated infringement procedures against Germany under Article 226 of the EC Treaty. The following year, the ECJ ruled that Germany had failed to fulfill its obligations under the RED and ordered it to pay the costs.[28] In June 2007, the Commission initiated the second step of infringement proceedings against 14 member states that it charged had not yet fully implemented the RED correctly, including Britain and France.

In 2006, the Grand Coalition finally enacted legislation that it chose to call an Equal Treatment Act rather than an Antidiscrimination Act. This came one year after the ECJ ruled that Germany had breached EU law by failing to transpose Directive 2000/43/EC.[29] The new law prohibits discrimination on all of the Article 13 grounds, namely race, ethnic background, gender, religion, world-view, disability, age, and sexual orientation. It is more limited than the Directives in terms of its scope. Larger trade associations feared that the law would confer a competitive disadvantage upon Germany. The Coalition accommodated some of their demands, and as a result, the scope of the law's application is narrower than the Directives require. Similarly, in order to appease the churches, the AGG allows religious communities, but not secular employers, to treat potential employees differently based upon their religious affiliation. This, too, falls short of EU law, which prohibits discrimination unless religious affiliation plays an *essential role* in the job. In terms of enforcement, the law does not accord NGOs a right to act on behalf of complainants. And, under the law, the Ministry of Family, Seniors, Women, and Youth in Berlin serves as the contact point for people who experience discrimination, but this body lacks the capacity to deal directly with cases and can only provide referrals to other institutions for concrete help.

6.7 CONCLUSION

In Britain and to a lesser extent in France, movement toward antidiscrimination laws existed. However, in Germany, "efforts to combat discrimination with legal means are predominantly based on European pressure to implement the Directives" (Baer 2005: 10). Bringing the spirit of these laws to bear upon social, economic, and governmental actors requires changing behavior through a variety of means. The RED emphasizes the availability of litigation as an ultimate means by which to make this happen. However, in order for litigation (or the threat of litigation) to work, the attitudes of a variety of actors must change. Individuals must be made aware of the law. Activists must be aware of the law. For the SLG, the adoption of European and national antidiscrimination laws was supposed to facilitate a new mode of advocacy. Yet, in France and Germany, lawyers largely perceived these laws as foreign intrusions that undermine traditional civil law, and they have yet to see legal action as a mean of advocacy. Moreover, lawyers and courts often lack expertise in antidiscrimination law.

In addition, judges must be receptive. As Latraverse (2007: 72) observes with regard to France, "Judicial actors in civil matters do not perceive rules of evidence as a central aspect of the civil judicial process and lack experience in making a systematic use of them...Meanwhile, the traditional formal theory of equality remains the ultimate reference and there is significant resistance to the concept of indirect discrimination." In France, "very few NGOs are knowledgeable in the management of judicial recourses" (Latraverse 2007: 7). Latraverse (2007: 72, note 131) observed that:

> In the field covered by the all anti-discrimination directives, including discrimination based on sex, there are only two NGOs specialised in bringing about legal action. The first is acting in the sector of sexual and moral harassment. It's name [is] AVFT. The second in the legal rights of foreigners: the GISTI. Generalist NGOs mostly intervene in penal actions, but do not focus their activity on legal actions.

Despite the transposition of most of the RED's terms in France and Germany, enforcement of the new law remained a problem. Sophie Latraverse (2007: 72) stated that: "More cases reach trial and are successful but they concern mainly direct discrimination in penal or labour cases on the ground of origin." Antidiscrimination policy still has to develop in these countries that are lacking the legal traditions of Britain and the U.S.

NOTES

* This chapter was written with Rhonda Evans Case.
1. Ladeur (2002).
2. Others have provided more comprehensive and detailed analyses of the compatibility of national law with the RED's requirement. For example, in 2002, the EUMC published a series of reports that compared each EU member state's existing anti-discrimination law with the RED. We do not seek to replicate their efforts here. By limiting our focus to five main elements of the Directive, we are able to provide a fuller analysis of the politics surrounding the RED's transposition. Such political analyses are thus far largely missing from the literature (cf. Amiya-Nakada 2007).
3. See *Mandla v. Lee* [1983] IRLR 209 (Lord Fraser of Tullybelton). British courts have interpreted the term "ethnic origins" or "ethnic group" to include Jews, Gypsies, and Irish Travelers, but not Muslims and Rastafarians.
4. See *King v. Great Britain China Centre* [1991] IRLR 513 and *Zafar v. Glasgow City Council* [1998] IRLR 36. In order to comply with the Burden of Proof Directive 97/80/EC, in 2001 the government introduced regulations to shift the burden of proof in cases involving sex discrimination in the areas of employment and vocational training (Statutory Instrument 2001 No. 2660 The Sex Discrimination (Indirect Discrimination and Burden of Proof) Regulations 2001).
5. Although France had three national administrative institutions with responsibilities that were linked in various ways to the issue of discrimination—namely, the High Council on Integration, the National Consultative Commission for Human Rights, and the Commissions on Access to Citizenship—none of these actually

performed all of the requisite functions of a national equality body as set forth in the RED.

6. This Network replaced the three previous specialized groups of experts that had focused on the grounds of racial and ethnic origin and religion, disability, and sexual orientation, and which had operated through June 2004.

7. The EUMC launched a call for tender process in May 2001 and selected the MPG to undertake this study.

8. Stephen Lawrence Inquiry (1999), *Report of an Inquiry by Sir William MacPherson of Cluny*, Cm 3684 (London: HMSO).

9. Race Relations (Amendment) Act 2000, s.19D.

10. The Race Relations (Immigration and Asylum) Authorization 2004 contains a list of nationalities that is not publicly available, and persons of these nationalities who seek to enter the country can be subjected to more rigorous examination than other persons, detention pending examination, refusal of leave to enter, and the imposition of other conditions (Cohen 2005: 35).

11. Hönekopp et al. (2002); Tikly (2004); Will (2003); and Will and Rühl (2004b).

12. See European Communities Act 1972, section 2(2).

13. Although our analysis does not cover other elements of the transposition in detail, we note that this two-track structure also applies to definitions of harassment and the exceptions for what constitutes a genuine occupational requirement (see Cohen 2005).

14. Some commentators contend that this new definition of indirect discrimination falls short of the RED (Cohen 2005: 17–18).

15. See Equality Act 2006.

16. "Combating Discrimination" ("*Lutter contre les discriminations*").

17. Equal Opportunities Act no. 2006-396 of March 31, 2006, art. 45, *JORF*, April 2, 2006.

18. CRIM 2006-16 E8/26-06-2006, *Bulletin officiel du Ministère de la Justice*, no. 102 (April 1 to June 30, 2006).

19. Hönekopp et al. (2002); Franchi (2004); Ebermeyer (2003); and Will and Rühl (2004).

20. In 2004, the European Commission initiated an infringement procedure against Germany in the ECJ (EIRO 2004). On April 28, 2005, the ECJ determined that Germany had breached its Treaty obligation in failing to transpose the Racial Equality Directive (Commission Press Release, IP/05/502), and on February 23, 2006 (OJ C 131/23, 3.6.2006), it determined that Germany had breached its Treaty obligation in failing to transpose the Employment Equality Directive. For both violations, it ordered Germany to pay costs.

21. "Germany: Citizenship, Asylum."

22. This new law entered into effect on January 1, 2000.

23. Hönekopp, Will, and Rühl (2002); Will and Rühl (2004); Will (2003); Will and Rühl (2004).

24. Stellungnahme von Pro Asyl e.V. zum Gesetzentwurf des BMJ (Stand 10. Dezember 2001) für ein "Gesetz zur Verhinderung von Diskriminierungen im Zivilrechtä," <http://cms.horus.be/files/99935/MediaArchive/pdf/Pro%20

Asyl%20zivilrechtliches%20ADG%202002-02-15.pdf>,   accessed   March 29, 2009.

25. Stellungnahme der Antidiskriminierungsinitiativen aus NRW zum Gesetzesentwurf Verhinderung von Diskriminierungen im Zivilrecht vom 10.12.01 (dated February 13, 2002), <http://cms.horus.be/files/99935/MediaArchive/pdf/ StellungnahmeNRW.pdf>, accessed March 29, 2009.

26. <http://cms.horus.be/files/99935/MediaArchive/pdf/germany2004_enOK.pdf>, pp. 16–17, accessed March 29, 2009.

27. EIRO (2004).

28. Case C-329/04: *Commission of the European Communities* v. *Federal Republic of Germany*, judgment of May 28, 2005) and Directive 2000/78/EC (Case C-43/05 *Commission* v. *Germany*, judgment of June 22, 2006).

29. <http://phpnuke.imir.de/modules.php?name=News&file=article&sid=103&mod e=&order=0&thold=0>, accessed June 2, 2006.

7

Retrenchment

7.1 FROM GROWTH AND SUCCESS TO SETBACKS

In the first few years after the transposition of the Equal Treatment Directives there was growth in both the number and staffing of the equality bodies and in some cases success in "naming and shaming" corporations and other entities for discrimination. The equality bodies were also somewhat successful in bringing awareness to the issues around discrimination. However, by the ten-year anniversary of the passage of the RED in 2010 it was clear that both politics and the European fiscal crisis were having a negative impact on the equality bodies.

Ten years after the passage of the RED many EU governments were slashing funding and moving once-independent entities into larger human rights bodies, thereby diluting their influence. The institutions created by the equality Directives were under fire partly because of the ongoing fiscal crisis, but also due to political pressure. The RED was a set of policies which developed along with European integration in the 1990s, but ran into the integration slowdown after enlargement in the mid-2000s and a lack of prioritization by mostly conservative governments. In this chapter, we continue our analysis of the impact of politics, focusing on the implementation of the equality Directives during a time of fiscal crisis for the EU. Using data from a 2010 survey distributed to EU equality bodies by staff of the Migration Policy Institute (MPI), we compare implementation and the impact of budget cuts. We also draw on material gathered during Equinet meetings in 2010 and 2011.

By 2008 most countries in the EU, including those that had recently joined, had passed laws implementing the EU's equality Directives. However, beginning in the mid-2000s the impact of radical right parties was being felt again, with electoral gains in countries like the Netherlands which put conservative politicians on the defensive. Most governments took a tough stance on issues of immigration control and began pushing for civic integration, an approach which emphasized language and civics education for immigrants, in some cases before they left their home country.

Ultimately antidiscrimination policy enforcement was put on the back burner. Britain's Labour government decided to merge the longstanding Commission for Race Equality into the Equality and Human Rights Commission, potentially blunting its impact in the area of racial discrimination. When the HALDE was created in France, most French people did not know it had been mandated by the EU, and some saw it as a "gift" from Chirac, along with the new Museum of Immigration which tried to highlight the positive side of France's immigration history. However, Nicolas Sarkozy took a dim view of the HALDE when he became president in 2005. Since the creation of the HALDE, litigation has increased, as shown in a study by Hermanin in which she states that "it is legitimate to affirm that the evolution of race antidiscrimination legislation has been crucially facilitated by the presence of an autonomous and comparatively powerful equality body endowed with competences to litigate" (Hermanin 2012: 13). Unfortunately the HALDE's success may be short-lived. After criticism came from the Sarkozy government, support for the HALDE was undermined through several politically motivated moves, including replacing the director, Louis Schweitzer, with an ally of Sarkozy, Jeannette Bougrab. Finally, the French Assembly passed a law in 2011 that folded the HALDE into a larger human rights entity, the *Defenseur des Droits*. Both staff from the HALDE and academic commentators expected this change to reduce the visibility, effectiveness, and power of the HALDE, particularly in the area of racial discrimination.

One of the early examples of politicization of an equality body was in Ireland, where the first head of that country's equality body ran afoul of the government. Niall Crowley, chief executive officer of Ireland's Equality Authority from 1999 to 2008, wrote a book, *Empty Promises* (2010), about his experiences and the politicization of implementation there. Ireland had passed equality legislation prior to the passage of the RED, in 1998 (under a left government), with seven grounds included: family status, age, disability, sexual orientation, race, religion, and Travellers. Two institutions were established by the Act to implement the legislation. The Equality Authority was responsible for combating discrimination and promoting equality of opportunity, providing information to the public, and reviewing the legislation for any necessary changes. The Equality Tribunal was created as a quasi-judicial body for those seeking redress under the equality legislation.

The Equality Authority faced criticism from the media when it went after Ryanair for age discrimination in 2001 and won. That criticism continued over the years, particularly when the Equality Authority went after pubs that refused to serve Travellers and also began to investigate allegations of discrimination in the public sector. After surviving various attempts at decentralization, comments from the Minister for Justice, Equality and Law Reform, Michael McDowell, who felt that "a dynamic liberal economy like ours demands flexibility and inequality in some respects to function" (Crowley 2010: 84), and even a near sacking, Crowley decided to resign in protest when he learned that the Authority's budget would be cut by 43 percent in 2008 and that there were plans to merge it with the Irish Human Rights Commission, and overall, losing much of its independence.

Crowley describes one of the key factors for the loss of support for antidiscrimination policy: "at a political level the enthusiasm for equality wanted. This was partly because of the influence of the Progressive Democrats [a business-oriented Liberal party], and in particular, Michael McDowell, Minister for Justice, Equality and Law Reform from 2002 to 2007, who was an articulate and forthright advocate of a more laissez-faire approach" (Crowley 2010: 112). Although Niall Crowley ended up resigning, he continued working with the European Commission on equality issues through Equinet, and was responsible for several reports evaluating the RED ten years after its passage.

The political attacks on the RED were not foreseen by the drafters of the Directive, and in any case there are few mechanisms besides the ECJ to deal with implementation. However, the equality bodies were created and in many cases even went beyond the mandate of the equality Directives. In the next section we will examine the development of the equality bodies and their competencies across the EU.

7.2 LEGISLATION IN PRACTICE: THE EU EQUALITY BODIES

The RED's most visible accomplishment was the creation of national equality bodies tasked with combating discrimination. The equality bodies have three principal goals: to assist and support victims to pursue complaints, to conduct independent surveys, and to publish independent reports on discrimination. The European Commission against Racism and Intolerance (ECRI) delineated the following competencies as central to a body's success:

- Providing aid and assistance to victims, including legal aid, and (where appropriate) to ensure victims have recourse to the courts or other judicial authorities.
- Monitoring the content and impact of legislation intended to combat racial discrimination, and recommending, where necessary, improvements to this legislation.
- Advising policy-makers on how to improve regulations and practices.
- Hearing complaints concerning specific cases of discrimination and seeking resolutions either through mediation or through binding and enforceable decisions.

- Sharing information with other national and European institutions tasked with promoting equality.
- Issuing advice on best practices of anti-discriminatory practice.
- Promoting public awareness of discrimination and disseminating pertinent information. (European Commission against Racism and Intolerance 1997)

The extension of antidiscrimination legislation—and the expansion of EU equality bodies—has the potential to greatly increase the efficiency and ability of EU states to combat all forms of discrimination. However, the effectiveness of these bodies is contingent on several factors, including: the breadth of their competencies; the tools at their disposal to enforce their rulings; their independence from state influences and control; and the financial resources available to adequately staff their operations and provide assistance to all victims. While the RED establishes a minimum standard for how EU member states should address discrimination complaints, this does not mean that EU citizens facing racial and ethnic discrimination will receive equal levels of assistance. Indeed, the competencies offered by equality bodies across the EU member states vary widely.

7.2.1 Mandate and Competencies

By 2010 not all states had instituted equality bodies—Estonia, Poland, and Slovenia, for example, did not have dedicated institutions in place to combat racial and ethnic discrimination.[1] Others do not have fully independent bodies (discussed in greater detail below), which means that the rulings of the body—as well as its budget—are accountable to a public organization. Others only instituted bodies between 2008 and 2010 (Czech Republic 2009, Luxembourg 2008, Spain 2009), and therefore do not have a long track record of hearing cases.

Some equality commissions have singular competencies whereas others provide a complete spectrum of assistance and information to citizens. Although not required by the RED, most member states offer a well-defined path for victims to resolve their complaint via a trial, mediation, or hearing. As EU law allows for member states to implement Directives as they see fit, three distinct paths to deliberation exist:

1. *Providing financial assistance.* One set of states, including the United Kingdom, offers to cover legal fees in selected situations to ensure that citizens are able to have their complaints heard in court despite financial limitations.

2. *Conducting hearings and issuing opinions.* Some states, like France and the Netherlands, have deliberative committees within their equality bodies that conduct hearings and offer opinions separate from the

national court system. The Bulgarian Commission for Protection against Discrimination functions as a quasi-court itself—and can impose sanctions—and therefore does not represent complainants in court.[2]

3. *Representing victims in court.* The Swedish Ombudsman is one example of an institution that also represents victims of discrimination free of charge in court.

The different structure of each body grants specific advantages and disadvantages. As noted above, some bodies act as quasi-judicial authorities (for instance in Bulgaria and the Netherlands), and thus refrain from offering services to victims or representing them in court in order to be seen as impartial. Therefore, although they may technically lack one of the key competencies—providing support to a victim while he or she seeks a resolution—this should not automatically be seen as a deficit. The Dutch equality body, for example, is considered one of the most effective because it delivers respected (though non-binding) opinions that are considered highly authoritative. However, it does not assist victims because this is seen to conflict with its primary aim of hearing and investigating cases (see European Union Agency for Fundamental Rights 2009, Annual Report).

Not only do the services of the equality commissions differ greatly, their mandates do as well. Some equality bodies do not address cases introduced by private institutions, employers, or individuals. The Ombudsman's office acts as the equality body in several nations (such as Greece), meaning that they mainly focus on instances of discrimination committed by public officials and offices. Furthermore, some equality bodies only cover certain cases

Table 7.1 Discrimination complaints registered in EU member states in 2007

	10–100		
	Bulgaria		
	Denmark		
	Greece		
	Hungary	100–500	
	Ireland	Austria	
	Latvia	Cyprus	More than 500
Fewer than 10	Lithuania	Finland	Belgium (1,691)
Estonia	Portugal	Germany	France (1,690)
Malta	Romania	Italy	Sweden (905)
Slovenia	Slovakia	Netherlands	United Kingdom (3,500)*

Source: European Union Agency for Fundamental Rights, Annual Report 2009.
* The UK data cover both 2006 and 2007.

of discrimination. For example, Malta's institution only provides assistance for those racially and ethnically discriminated against in regard to the provision of goods and services. This is a particular problem because the bulk of discriminatory incidents do not occur in the public sector (which is increasingly well monitored). According to the EU-MIDIS survey, discrimination in "private services" dominates individuals' experiences of discrimination in the EU-27, followed by work-related discrimination.[3]

Finally, the wide range in the number of complaints received by each body (see Table 7.1) provides another method of comparison, although these data can be misleading. Fewer registered complaints should not be taken as evidence of less discrimination in those countries; it is more likely an indication of the underutilization of these bodies, primarily because victims are either unaware that they exist or otherwise reluctant to seek their services.

7.2.2 Independence

Though almost all equality bodies claim that they act independently and impartially when dealing with discrimination issues, the links between some of the bodies and federal institutions could potentially undermine their impartiality. For example, Austria's Ombudsman for Equal Treatment is attached to the Federal Chancellery, and Belgium's equality body has a board run entirely by government officials. Furthermore, the Spanish body that conducts reports and recommendations is actually a subsection of the Ministry of Immigration and Employment. While these organizational structures do not by themselves compromise the work of the equality bodies, the bodies' close affiliation with government ministries presents a potential conflict of interest. And even the perception of partiality may diminish the effectiveness of these bodies, as victims may feel less comfortable seeking their help.

Another area of concern is consolidation and reorganization. As equality bodies have made decisions which are unpopular with government officials, there have been threats to dilute their influence by moving them into larger entities within the government bureaucracy. This could affect both the impact and independence of an equality body. In some countries, the groups tasked with equality are housed within institutions with larger mandates, such as the Ombudsman's office. This means that the specialized expertise needed to adjudicate discrimination complaints could potentially be lost, or simply not prioritized, within the larger institution—especially during times of budget cuts. Similarly, in countries such as Lithuania, multiple bodies, each with a specialized mandate (for instance, gender equality, children's rights, and racial discrimination), are being consolidated into one. Again, the fear is that the emphasis on discrimination would be lost.

7.3 POLITICS AND BUDGET CUTS

Most of the equality bodies are in their infancy as institutions, and thus have been going through a growing period of structural changes, consolidation, and gradual increases of capacity. While some have continued to expand, per their original strategic missions, budget and staff cuts have affected several others. This information must be presented with the caveat that the budget figures alone do not necessarily allow us to compare actual antidiscrimination expenditures across member states. Some bodies with larger budgets may cover multiple grounds, or be housed within institutions with different mandates, and thus actually spend less on discrimination than smaller institutions who devote a larger proportion of their resources to covering ethnic and racial discrimination. We face the same problem of measurement when we look at staff numbers. For example, the Greek Ombudsman has an impressive 142 staff members, but only 15 deal with discrimination, putting it on par with Denmark's eight-person staff—one of the smallest.

As Table 7.2 and Figure 7.1 show, budgets decreased substantially for at least three equality bodies between 2008 and 2009: both Ireland and Lithuania saw dramatic decreases of over 40 percent,[4] while Latvia and Romania followed with 30 and 25 percent cuts, respectively.

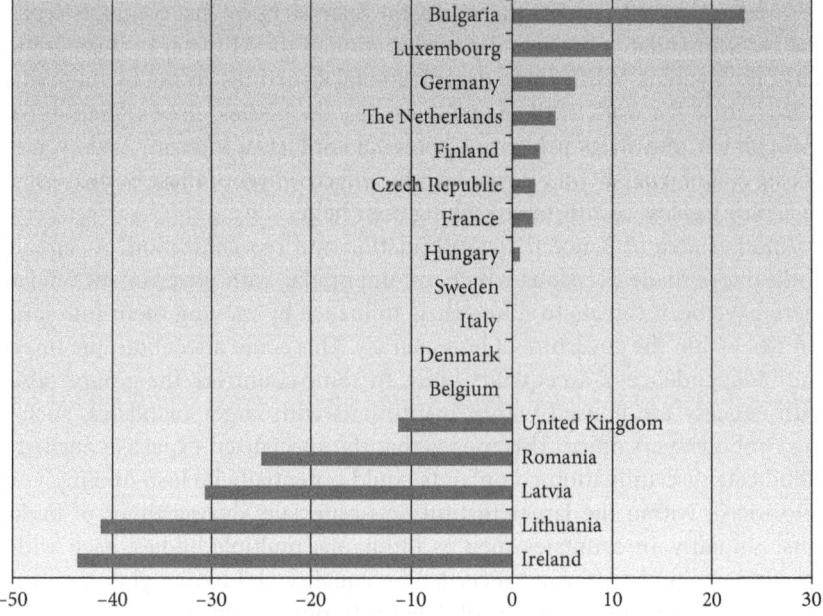

Figure 7.1 Percentage change in budgets of EU equality bodies, 2008–2009
Source: MPI questionnaires to EU equality bodies.

Table 7.2 Budgets of equality bodies in EU member states (in euros)

	Budget 2008	Budget 2009	Percentage Change
Ireland	5,897,000	3,333,000	–43.48
Lithuania	538,114	316,555	–41.17
Latvia	1,855,068	1,287,016	–30.62
Romania	*	*	–25**
United Kingdom	88,287,759	78,305,119	–11.31
Belgium	7,500,000	7,500,000	0
Denmark	806,024	806,024	0
Greece***	*	10,269,000	*
Malta	256,000	256,000	0
Italy	2,035,000	2,035,000	0
Sweden	9,360	9,360	0
Hungary	972,895	980,294	0.76
France	11,600,000	11,837,000	2.04
Czech Republic	3,712,630	3,797,449	2.28
Finland	685,082	704,000	2.76
The Netherlands	*	*	4.30
Germany	2,814,000	2,990,000	6.25
Luxembourg	200,000	220,000	10.00
Bulgaria	1,338,211	1,650,000	23.30

* Exact figures unavailable; equality bodies only reported the percent change from 2008–2009.
** This figure comes from news reports, as Romania did not respond to the questionnaire.
*** Although data do not exist for Greece prior to 2009, they announced a budget decrease for 2010.
Note: National currencies have been converted to euros using the exchange rates from July 1, 2009.
Source: MPI questionnaires to EU equality bodies.

Other indicators that agencies were looking for ways to make further cuts include the fact that five equality bodies asked for waivers of the fee they pay to be part of the European Network of Equality Bodies (Equinet); alarmed by these cutbacks, the network launched campaigns reminding governments that they are legally required to maintain their equality bodies.

In some countries, such as the United Kingdom, budget cuts coincided with a reduction in staff levels. At the same time, the demands on these institutions—and their caseloads—are growing. The UK equality body (the Equality and Human Rights Commission) reports a 10 percent increase in its caseload in the field of human rights, which represents a new area of responsibility for the organization (in addition to the multiple equality strands it covers). This has garnered accusations of the institution being stretched too thin: the

ECRI has raised concerns that the EHRC's current budget "may not suffice to maintain previous levels of protection against racism" (European Commission against Racism and Intolerance 2010). Other bodies have also reported burgeoning caseloads without any significant increases in capacity. The French anti-discrimination and equality body HALDE received 10,546 complaints in 2009—a drastic jump from just 1,500 complaints in 2005, and a solid 21 percent increase from the number of complaints received in 2008. Yet they report "stagnation" in terms of recruitment, with an expected addition of only two staff members in 2010, potentially impeding their ability to handle the new caseload.[5] The Hungarian Equal Treatment Authority's budget increased slightly from 2008 to 2009, but it also accompanied an increased caseload. While four lawyers were added to the staff in 2008 "due to added burdens," the body reports that its current staff size is not sufficient to handle the number of complaints in a timely fashion.[6]

In Bulgaria, the caseload of the Bulgarian Commission for Protection against Discrimination has shot up to 1,039 complaints in 2009, compared to 714 in 2008 (more than half relating to labor discrimination). While the Commission reports recent increases in staff (including legal advisers) and budget to deal with the growing number of cases,[7] the government has approved a recommendation to cut expenses by reducing the numbers of members on the anti-discrimination commission from nine to five (the body serves the role of a tribunal in adjudicating discrimination cases). NGO critics claimed this move, justified by state budget cuts due to the financial crisis, would seriously limit the Commission's capacity to review discrimination claims, and would result in long delays in hearing cases.[8] Similarly, in Romania budget cuts have left the National Council for Combating Discrimination in limbo, with four out of nine members of the Council finishing their terms with no replacements (the Council also plays a tribunal role and needs a minimum of five members to decide cases).[9]

While the recession may have contributed to halting the expansion of some bodies—especially in the countries most affected by the downturn—other countries' budgets have stayed the same or increased, with others expected to rise in 2010, in line with the overall growth strategies of these new agencies. In Denmark, the budget figure has remained unchanged since 2003 (at 6 million Danish Kroner, or approximately €800,000). Some bodies have reported increases in staff (including the number of lawyers assigned to review complaints). And in some countries, we can even observe positive trends in terms of oversight. In the Czech Republic, increased public scrutiny of how the government has dealt with foreign workers during the crisis—including the voluntary return program—may have led to a pressure for increased oversight of antidiscrimination measures. In a 2009 report to the European Migration Network, the Czech National Contact Point reported that regional problems arising from the dismissal of foreign workers during the economic crisis led the Ministry of the Interior to create "emergent integration projects" in selected municipalities to "improve the quality of coexistence of immigrants and the majority society, and prevent xenophobia" (European Migration Network 2010: 30). While not directly linked to the economic crisis, another positive development occurred in June 2009 when the Czech Parliament became the last EU member state to pass antidiscrimination legislation, which had been vetoed just one year prior—thus coming into compliance with the RED and avoiding EU sanctions (Boučková 2009).

7.3.1 Key Challenges

While the very existence of these bodies—and in some cases their growth—is an example of the significant progress made in legislation, this has not always translated into progress on the ground. In a recent analysis, the Romanian Center for Juridical Resources (CRJ) attests that equality in Romania is a "principle that exists solely on paper," and that the country has regressed in its efforts to combat discrimination since its 2007 accession to the EU. On paper, Romania complies with EU-mandated legislation, but the CRJ contends that in reality, public officials do not bother to document or adjudicate discrimination complaints, and only 15.7 percent of local authorities believe that vulnerable groups (particularly people with disabilities, the unemployed, and Roma) receive adequate protections.[10]

Lack of awareness is another huge obstacle to the effectiveness of these bodies. The EU-MIDIS survey shows that even when individuals were prompted with the names of the equality bodies in their country of residence, 63 percent say they have not heard of any of them. When asked a more open-ended question—if they knew of any organization that offered support to people who are discriminated against—only 16 percent said they did (European Union Agency for Fundamental Rights 2009: 13). This helps explain why 82 percent of those discriminated against did not report their experience either at the place where it occurred (for instance work or school) or to a competent authority. The most common reason given by all respondents for not reporting incidents of discrimination was the belief that "nothing would happen" if they told authorities; the third most commonly cited reason for not reporting was simply not knowing how to do so (European Union Agency for Fundamental Rights 2009).

Equality bodies are still nascent institutions and have undergone major changes in the past five years, including consolidations spurred by recent tweaks in EU legislation. This stage of development makes them especially vulnerable; which in turn makes their operations more sensitive to recession-induced effects, such as budget cuts. While they are now more critical than ever, they

are also in a fragile stage of development, where more resources and evalua-
tion are paramount to their success.

The main challenges facing the EU equality bodies include the following:

- *Reduction of resources.* The effectiveness of many new bodies has been
  impeded by cuts to institutional budgets, legal funds, and the number of
  staff assigned to cases. In some cases, the mandates of the equality bodies have been extended without a corresponding increase in resources,
  impeding their ability to engage in the critical mass of work necessary to
  be effective.

- *Restructuring.* While in past years many member states had distinct institutions responsible for different aspects of equality, a period of consolidation has meant that bodies have been merged with other organizations.
  The risk is that the specific expertise and resources dedicated to combating discrimination could be lost within the larger structure.

- *Threats to independence.* The antidiscrimination functions of many bodies have been merged with other bureaucracies, which could lead to a
  dilution of their influence. Making key appointments (like commissioners on equality authorities) contingent on political will and/or government financing is also problematic.

- *Lack of expertise.* The equality bodies should mitigate their lack of experience by sharing good practices with other equality bodies in networks
  such as Equinet. They also need to work to ensure that those who benefit
  from this legislation are also aware of it.

Studies done of the equality bodies in 2010, as part of the ten-year review of
the equality Directives, provide a mixed picture on the implementation
of the equality Directives. An Equinet report on the powers and practices
of equality bodies from 2010 notes that "there is great variation in regard to
how often these powers are made use of in practice and...the potential of
these powers in regard to having an impact on the development of law is not
always utilized fully" (Equinet 2010: 32). Equality bodies vary in the scope
of actions that they can take and a clear issue cited in reports has been that
of communicating the existence of the laws to affected groups: "Few states
are considered to have adequately transposed the Directives' requirements
to disseminate information on discrimination laws, to promote social dialogue and to encourage dialogue with non-governmental organisations"
(Chopin and Do 2011: 9). This lack of communication was also evident in a
survey done by the EU's Fundamental Rights Agency (FRA) in 2009, which
stated:

> This survey provides evidence that the groups most vulnerable to discrimination
> in the EU remain uninformed about legislation forbidding discrimination against
> people on the basis of their ethnicity. On average, 43% of respondents (depending

on the group and the area of discrimination) thought that no anti-discrimination legislation existed, and a further 20% were unsure.[11]

A study of the implementation of the RED by the FRA in 2012 indicates that many of the challenges discussed in this chapter remain. Despite many positive examples of implementation of the equality Directives, the lack of awareness among racial minorities and social partners in the EU "affects the degree to which victims pursue their rights" (FRA 2012: 25). The report calls for raising awareness and targeting persons who belong to groups most at risk of discrimination, since the effectiveness of remedies is "undermined where victims are reluctant to use them. Several factors have been noted that act as a disincentive to using complaints procedures: legal costs; fear of negative consequences; a perception that the situation would not alter; a tolerance of or failure to recognize discrimination" (FRA 2012: 25).

7.4 CONCLUSION

The principal issue related to discrimination in Europe today is no longer the lack of legislation, but rather its uneven implementation on the ground. While satisfactory—and increasingly comprehensive—legislation to combat discrimination is in place in almost all EU member states, it has not been implemented to full advantage. In many cases, implementation has simply been "pro forma," meaning that otherwise adequate legislative measures have been undermined by a lack of political will and public support.

More recent actions show that the trend toward cuts and consolidation continues. The French HALDE has been consolidated into the office of the "Défenseur des Droits" which has the following four mandates:

- protects the rights and freedoms in the context of relations with government;
- defends and promotes the interests and rights of the child;
- fights against discrimination prohibited by law and promoting equality;
- enforces ethics by persons engaged in security activities.[12]

Those who worked at the HALDE prior to the transition feared that their work would get lost in a larger institution with multiple mandates. In the UK, the *Guardian* newspaper reported that the "budget of the Equality and Human Rights Commission has been cut by 63%" and the *Daily Mail* reported in late March 2012 that Trevor Phillips, the head of the EHRC since 2006 when the organization was created, was stepping down.

The global economic downturn has been perceived to be a "trigger" for increased intolerance and discrimination against migrants and members of minority groups, exacerbated by budget cuts and waning political will to combat it. However, this is likely to be a temporary spike that does not yet indicate an increase in institutional discrimination. However, this does point to the need for governments to act quickly: the right measures need to be put in place during countries' recovery period from the crisis to stave off a worsening of the situation of migrants and minorities—groups already at risk.

In light of these challenges, the European Union's antidiscrimination priority for the next decade should not be to create more legislation or more institutions; instead, the EU needs to strengthen the ones it already has. European governments, EU institutions, and civil society partners need to come together to evaluate what is working and what is not, and to reinforce the existing structures.

NOTES

* This chapter was written with research support from Natalia Banulescu, Migration Policy Institute.

1. As of 2010, Estonia had a Gender Equality Commissioner, but no institution that deals with discrimination on the grounds of race or ethnicity; Poland had no independent equality body, though there is a Department of Women, Family and Counteracting Discrimination within the Ministry of Labour and Social Policy.
2. Bulgarian questionnaire.
3. EU-MIDIS defines "private services" as those an individual might encounter in the following situations: trying to open a bank account or obtaining a loan, entering or patronizing a shop, restaurant, bar, or café. See: European Union Agency for Fundamental Rights 2009, Data in Focus Report 1: The Roma, 5.
4. Niall Crowley, then chief of Ireland's Equality Authority, resigned in protest over these cuts in October 2008.
5. MPI questionnaire from the French High Commission against Discrimination and for Equality (HALDE).
6. MPI questionnaire from the Hungarian Equal Treatment Authority.
7. MPI questionnaire submitted by the Bulgarian Commission for Protection against Discrimination.
8. <http://www.state.gov/g/drl/rls/hrrpt/2009/eur/136024.htm>, accessed May 3, 2010.
9. "Ireland leads cuts on equality bodies." *Village Magazine*, March 2, 2010. <http://www.theormond.ie/villagemagazine/?p=167>.
10. "Lupta Antidiscriminare, Uitata pe Hartie dupa Integrare," *Evenimentual Zilei*, March 8, 2010.
11. <http://fra.europa.eu/fraWebsite/eu-midis/eumidis_main_results_report_en.htm>, accessed August 8, 2012.
12. Translated by Terri Givens from the website: <http://www.defenseurdesdroits.fr/connaitre-son-action>, accessed October 8, 2012.

8

Conclusion: A Comparison to the U.S. and the Future of Antidiscrimination Policy in Europe*

8.1 INTRODUCTION

The preceding chapters have provided a detailed analysis of the development of antidiscrimination policy in the European Union with a focus on Britain, France, and Germany. We began the book by examining the discourses that impacted the development of antidiscrimination policy in Europe. These discourses helped to trace the shift from a focus on anti-racism to a focus on antidiscrimination policy. Key actors helped with the shift, particularly the SLG and European Commission. However, once the RED was passed, the legislation and policy ran into new hurdles that have impacted implementation.

The analysis of the equality Directives is a complex undertaking. However, we have shown that the starting points of each country had an impact on both the negotiations and transposition of the RED. We have also shown that the development of the Directives cannot be explained solely by intergovernmental or neo-functionalist theories. The factors influencing the passage of antidiscrimination policy were many, and did not necessarily align with theories developed by other authors.

This analysis demonstrates the strength of an institutionalist approach, utilizing process tracing to clearly identify the development over time of a policy process that led to an outcome that may have been unexpected, given the positions of the member states. By bring in rational choice institutionalism and focusing on the strategic actions of individuals, we show how these actions impacted the agenda-setting at the EU level. However, perhaps our main added value is in analyzing the development of the discourses over time, and how this was both an indicator of the direction of policy, and ultimately the outcome of policy-making.

Throughout the development of Article 13, it is clear that the issue of immigration was an important factor in the recommendations that were made by the various reports like those of the Ford and Kahn Commissions. There is ample evidence that key figures within the SLG saw the campaign for an antidiscrimination Directive as a means of addressing migrants' issues. For example, for Jan Niessen, who served as director of the MPG and chair of the SLG, a racial Directive represented a "new instrument to promote the societal integration of established immigrant communities and racial or ethnic minorities" (Niessen 1998).[1] And, Isabelle Chopin (1999c: 113), who replaced Niessen as the MPG's director and who also chaired the SLG, maintained that "the absence of an effective and concerted fight against the rise of racism and xenophobia seriously destabilizes and undermines the different social integration processes set up in the Union Member States."

However, it is also clear that much of what the SLG wanted in regards to immigration and TCNs did not come to fruition. Member states still retain a great deal of sovereignty, particularly over the comings and goings of non-EU citizens. Although the RED represented a major development for ethnic minorities, a great deal of work remains in the area of rights for TCNs. Although the RED got its start in debates surrounding immigration and race, in the end it remains a limited approach to issues of discrimination.

So the question remains: whither antidiscrimination policy in Europe? The EU has held annual "Equality Summits" in order to examine issues around inequality and discrimination, with participants discussing best practices but with few concrete measures coming from the meetings. Other entities such as the Migration Policy Group and Equinet continue to lobby and organize to keep antidiscrimination policy on the agenda. As these policies continue to evolve, it is interesting to compare policy development in the U.S. and Europe, and how specific approaches, such as strategic litigation, may be utilized to advance the cause of antidiscrimination.

8.2 ANTIDISCRIMINATION LAWS IN THE UNITED STATES AND EUROPE COMPARED

The United States and the EU have served as the basis for many fruitful comparisons, particularly of the public law variety (see Shapiro and Stone Sweet 2002). The U.S. has a long history of antidiscrimination law, and as with the EU, antidiscrimination law has played a pivotal role in the evolution of its federal system.

8.2.1 U.S. Antidiscrimination Policy

From its founding, race and law have been integral components of state- and nation-building processes in the United States. Slavery, in effect, transformed people into property, and elaborate rules governed the existence of blacks, free and slave, in the North as well as the South. Even after the institution of slavery was destroyed by a bloody civil war, whites continued to use law as a means of subjugating African Americans. As a result, an array of state and federal legal systems, often known by the euphemism "Jim Crow," codified various racial distinctions, often limiting the capacity of African Americans to vote or to enter into contracts, the two fundamental elements of participation in a Lockean democracy. In addition, under the common law, owners of property and capital essentially possessed a right to discriminate. They could thus refuse services, accommodation, and employment to individuals on any grounds. This right gave whites, particularly white men, considerable non-state power to shape communities.

The first antidiscrimination statutes date back to the Civil War era. They were part of an effort to incorporate free blacks into state and national polities. Unsurprisingly, the state of Massachusetts, an abolitionist stronghold, enacted the first such law—on May 16, 1865. It prohibited discrimination on grounds of color or race in certain public places and provided that violations be punished by a fine not exceeding 50 dollars.[2] At the federal level, antidiscrimination statutes were part of a state-building effort (Foner 1990). In 1875, just before the political demise of the Radical Republicans, Congress adopted "An Act to Protect All Citizens in Their Civil and Legal Rights" (hereinafter "Civil Rights Act of 1875") (see Foner 1990: 226–27, 233–34, 247). Although it was part of the Republicans' broader effort to reconstruct the American South, the Act applied to the entire nation, prohibiting discrimination on grounds of race, color, or previous condition of servitude in the use of inns, public conveyances, and other places of public amusement.[3] Violators were liable to criminal and civil penalties in the federal courts, and aggrieved individuals retained the prerogative to seek redress under the common law or according to state statutes, where those existed. In the reactionary period that followed, however, the U.S. Supreme Court struck down the Civil Rights Act of 1875, holding that Congress had exceeded the scope of the federal government's powers under the Constitution.[4] No further congressional action on racial discrimination was taken until 1957.[5]

In 1954, the U.S. Supreme Court's landmark decision in *Brown* v. *Board of Education* made headlines around the world. In its wake, a newly galvanized civil rights movement emerged, culminating with the contrasting images of police brutality in Selma, Mississippi in 1965 and a peaceful gathering on the Washington Mall in 1963. The Civil Rights Act of 1964 and the Voting Rights Act of 1965 consolidated a patchwork of judicial and state-based reforms and articulated national civil rights standards enforceable through the federal courts.

8.2.2 Comparative Themes

In the U.S., the first antidiscrimination laws addressed racial discrimination, whereas sex discrimination was the subject of the EU's first antidiscrimination laws. In 1957, the founding document of the European Community, the Treaty of Rome, now Article 141 (formerly 119)[6] of the present Treaty Establishing the European Community (TEC) created a basic guarantee of equal pay for equal work between the sexes. At the time, French laws on equal pay were more advanced than those of its Treaty partners. Fearing that its laws would put French industries at a competitive disadvantage within the common market, France insisted on the inclusion of this provision in the Treaty (Barnard 1996). Since then, EU efforts in the area of gender discrimination have been substantial. By contrast, Virginia Senator Howard W. Smith added sex as a protected class to the Civil Rights Act of 1964 in an attempt to divide the bill's supporters (Whalen and Whalen 1985).

Historically, the demographic composition of the European countries vis-à-vis the U.S. differs in important respects. America's African American population is the legacy of slavery. To a lesser extent, the southwest contained Latino populations that were incorporated into the U.S. by virtue of the Treaty of Guadalupe-Hildago in 1848. By contrast, immigration flows into Europe from colonial sources did not accelerate until the 1960s. Thus, racially diverse groups comprise a smaller proportion of the population in European countries, with great variance among them in terms of both numbers and the origins of the immigrants.

In the U.S., strong civil society organizations had developed around the issue of race, e.g., the National Association for the Advancement of Colored People (NAACP), the Congress of Racial Equalitly (CORE), the Southern Christian Leadership Conference (SCLC), etc., whereas women's organizations were still in a nascent stage by the mid-1960s. The SLG is similar in some ways to the coalition of American interest groups that lobbied for U.S. civil rights legislation in the early 1960s under an umbrella group known as the Leadership Conference on Civil Rights. However, the SLG did not have the same kind of support from a social movement. Although immigrant rights groups were involved with the SLG, immigrants themselves were not mobilized in the same way African Americans and their white supporters were in the U.S.

The EU and U.S. both confronted important constitutional issues in their pursuit of antidiscrimination legislation. The European Parliament acted to put EU-wide antidiscrimination legislation on the political agenda in 1986 with its creation of the Parliamentary Inquiry Committee, charged with examining the rise of fascism and racism in Europe. However, at that time, the European Treaty did not provide a legal basis for the adoption of a legislative instrument addressing those phenomena. In 1992, the Starting Line Group began campaigning for both antidiscrimination legislation and the inclusion of an antidiscrimination provision in the European Treaty. As we have shown, radical right parties' anti-immigrant discourses and violence against immigrants played a key role in motivating the actions of the SLG.

The U.S. also experienced a reactionary movement against federal antidiscrimination laws. It erupted with the 1948 election. In response to President Harry S. Truman's signals of a new liberalism on civil rights issues, Strom Thurmond and a band of renegade Democrats, formally known as the States Rights Party but colloquially known as the "Dixiecrats," ran their own presidential campaign. They won several Southern states, foreshadowing a breakdown in the New Deal coalition. In 1964, U.S. Senator Barry Goldwater won some of those same states in his ill-fated contest for the presidency, and Alabama Governor George C. Wallace also enjoyed electoral success there.

There is clearly more work to be done in comparing the development of antidiscrimination policy in the U.S. and Europe, particularly as the strategy of strategic litigation moves forward. However, it is clear that there were several key factors that motivated policy in both Europe and the U.S. First, violence and discrimination against ethnic minorities and the development of anti-minority political groups clearly motivated policy developments in both cases. However, strategic litigation played a greater role in the development of policy in the U.S., whereas it appears to be playing a greater role in the implementation of policy in Europe.

8.2.3 Support for Strategic Litigation

As we have shown,[7] the RED was supported by a coalition of migrant activists and legal experts that was known as the Starting Line Group. The SLG pursued a Directive that would facilitate access to courts so that litigation could be used as an alternative means through which to advance their policy interests. Key figures within the SLG recognized that a Directive alone would not transform civil society's capacity to make use of the RED and the national legislation that it spawned. For example, as Anne Dummett acknowledged, "lawyers and organizations were thin on the ground in many member states."[8] In order to exploit the opportunities presented by the new antidiscrimination laws, community activists would require training so that they could recognize behavior as constituting unlawful discrimination, and lawyers would require training in order to initiate and manage antidiscrimination litigation. Following the RED's adoption, organizations that had belonged to the SLG drew upon a variety of transnational and supranational resources in order to develop civil society's antidiscrimination enforcement capacity. A couple of examples illustrate their interests in this regard and the resources that they exploited in order to promote these interests.

In January 2001, the European Roma Rights Centre, Interights, and the Migration Policy Group launched what would become a joint six-year project, designated "Strategies on Litigation Tackling Discrimination in EU Countries" (SOLiD; Interights 2004: 11). The partners sought to support local and regional groups in maximizing the "historic opportunity" presented by the RED, and were ultimately joined by the Northern Ireland Council for Ethnic Minorities (Lead Partner), the European Network against Racism (Core Partner), the Columbia Law School Public Interest Law Initiative, the National Bureau against Racial Discrimination (*Landelijk Bureau ter bestrijding van Rassendiscriminatie*—LBR), and the Documentation and Advisory Centre on Racial Discrimination (DRC/DACoRD).[9]

The MPG had been a key supporter of the RED and advocated for provisions that would facilitate access to the courts, thus its activity in this regard could be expected. The ERRC and Interights were organizations that themselves made use of strategic litigation. The ERRC, which had been established in 1996, was an international public interest law organization that sought to combat anti-Romani racism and human rights abuses,[10] and Interights was a British organization established in 1982 "to promote and protect human rights through the use of law and legal institutions" (Interights 2003: 5). The SOLiD project consisted of convening workshops for activists, politicians, government officials, judges, and lawyers; litigation; and the lobbying of governments. With support from George Soros' Open Society Institute and the European Network against Racism (ENAR), it produced a 200-page book entitled *Strategic Litigation of Race Discrimination in Europe: From Principles to Practice (A Manual on the Theory and Practice of Strategic Litigation with Particular Reference to the EC Race Directive)*. This book became the guide for the training of potential litigators across the European Union.

Acknowledging that the large number of victims of discrimination and limited access to justice will mean that litigation cannot be pursued in every case, SOLiD advocated for the use of "strategic litigation" (Interights 2003: 12). Tansy Hutchinson, a Policy Officer with ENAR, described the SOLiD project in the following terms: "It was about trying to enable NGOs ... to look at strategic litigation." She explained that: "Rather than just bringing every case that comes to the door," strategic litigation involves picking cases that will set "a precedent that will influence the next twenty [cases] that come along" (Hutchinson 2007: 77–78). The project emphasized the importance of strengthening ties between NGOs and lawyers, a task that was easier in some countries, where NGOs already employed lawyers, than in others, where lawyers and activists had to be brought together and trust had to be developed. This, Hutchinson explained, would "contribute to effective transposition and implementation of the directive" (Hutchinson 2007: 77–78).

In subsequent years, a number of legal seminars were convened across Europe, all with the intention of cultivating civil society's awareness of the new antidiscrimination laws and its capacity to make use of them. In addition, the Human European Consultancy, in partnership with the MPG, carried out a project for the European Commission on "Mapping Capacity of Civil Society

Dealing with Anti-discrimination."[11] The project was intended to develop the capacity of civil society in the new member states and Bulgaria, Romania, and Turkey to deal with antidiscrimination. Two-day national seminars, targeting local representatives from NGOs, were held in each of the 13 countries during June 2005. These seminars focused on the role of NGOs in combating discrimination on the grounds of racial or ethnic origin, age, disability, religion or belief, and sexual orientation. The program dealt with the concepts of discrimination as set out in the EU Directives 2000/43 and 2000/78 and aimed at "awareness raising, dialogue with the government, support to victims and litigation in the context of the national situation of government legislation and policies."[12]

For example, in June 2007, the European Union Agency for Fundamental Rights organized seminars in Croatia and Turkey. The initiative, which had been launched in 2006 by the agency's predecessor, the European Monitoring Centre on Racism and Xenophobia, was aimed at supporting the capacity of governmental and non-governmental institutions, agencies, and associations in both countries to collect and analyze data related to ethnic or racial discrimination. The RED served as a focus of these seminars. A summary of the Istanbul proceedings was subsequently published and made available online. It was produced with the financial assistance of the European Commission's Directorate General for Enlargement Program. Two of the presentations promoted the idea of strategic litigation. These included one by Andi Dobrushi (2007), a Senior Staff Attorney at the ERRC, entitled "Testing the Enforcement of Anti-discrimination Laws in Europe: Selected ERRC Cases." The second was by Tansy Hutchinson (2007), Policy Officer (and lawyer) at the ENAR. She had worked as a trainer with the SOLiD project, and her presentation examined the role of NGOs, particularly with regard to providing litigation support and engaging in strategic litigation.

In November 2008, the European Commission's Employment, Social Affairs and Equal Opportunities DG (2008: 27) sponsored a legal seminar in Brussels on the implementation of EU law on equal opportunities and antidiscrimination. It was coordinated by the MPG, and Jan Niessen, a key figure within the SLG, served as the seminar's Chair. This seminar included a panel entitled, "Enforcement and the Role of Equality Bodies: Best Practices?" According to the discussion paper for this panel, "the targeted litigation policy of the U.S. Equal Employment Opportunity Commission in the early 1970s demonstrates the potential of [strategic litigation], as it had a significant result in 'identifying and breaking down patterns of systemic race and sex discrimination and shaping much of the core legal concepts in discrimination law'" (2008: 27, quoting Holtmaat 2006: 55).

The emphasis on strategic litigation highlights the ongoing role of transnational activists in the implementation of the RED. It also highlights the lessons learned from the U.S. example.

8.3 CONCLUSION

It is commonly acknowledged that the EU is an elite construction. It is paradoxical that elites have turned to race policy as one avenue for cultivating popular support for that construction. Ideas about race and national identity underlie right-wing rhetoric as do fears about unaccountable elites that impose their preferences upon a potentially unwilling populace. The RED developed as the response of left-leaning politicians to the rise of radical right parties, but it is clear that implementation has not been as straightforward as hoped by the activists who supported the measure. The EU will continue to face these kinds of challenges as it ventures into policy areas that impact social issues that are still very much contested in many countries.

Radical right parties continue to play a role in European politics, as seen in the rise of Geert Wilders in the Netherlands, and the support for Marine Le Pen in the 2012 French presidential election. Whether this will lead to more support for antidiscrimination policy remains to be seen; the fiscal crisis in Europe has led to a diminished focus on the plight of ethnic minorities, despite a clear need for support during difficult times.

Clearly there will be many interesting developments as the implementation of the equality Directives moves forward. As the world works through a period of economic crisis, many issues will arise regarding ethnic minorities and immigration. Many countries will also face new challenges with their ethnic minority populations, as they begin to develop their own political voices. The election of Barack Obama in the United States has led to elites in Europe questioning their own prospects for electing a non-white politician to lead their countries. Researchers will need to work across disciplines in order to make sense of new political and social developments in Europe. We hope that this book is a step in that direction.

NOTES

* This chapter was written with Rhonda Evans Case.
1. Niessen (1998).
2. Mass. Stat. 1865, ch. 277, sec. 1, 2; Laws of Mass., 1864–65, at 650.
3. 18 Stat. 335, sec. 1 (1875).
4. *Civil Rights Cases*, 109 U.S. 3 (1883).
5. The Civil Rights Act of 1957 was a weak measure and primarily addressed voting rights. It was not until the Civil Rights Act of 1964 that Congress again attempted to regulate non-governmental discrimination.

6. The Treaty of Amsterdam renumbered and amended former Article 119 of the Treaty of Rome. As a result, the new Article 141 extends the definition of equal pay for equal work by reference to "or work of equal value."
7. See also Evans Case and Givens (2010).
8. Personal correspondence, January 11, 2006.
9. <http://www.solid-eu.org/index.php>, accessed April 2, 2009.
10. See <http://www.errc.org/About_index.php>, accessed May 17, 2005.
11. See <http://www.migpolgroup.com/portfolio/mapping-capacity-of-civil-society-dealing-with-anti-discrimination/> for a link to a report, accessed November 14, 2013.
12. See <http://ec.europa.eu/employment_social/fundamental_rights/civil/map_en.htm>, accessed January 10, 2009.

Bibliography

Amiya-Nakada, Ryosuke. 2007. "Transposition Strategy and Political Time in the Europeanisation of Social Norms: Comparing Transposition of the Anti-discrimination Directives in Germany and Austria." Paper presented for the fourth General Conference of the European Consortium for Political Research, Pisa, Italy, September 6–8. Available at <http://aei.pitt.edu/7570/1/PP517.pdf>. Accessed November 11, 2013.

Armony, Ariel C. and Victor Armony. 2009. "Indictments, Myths, and Citizen Mobilization in Argentina: A Discourse Analysis." In *Latin American Democratic Transformations: Institutions, Actors, and Processes*, ed. William C. Smith. Malden, MA: Wiley-Blackwell, 319–38.

Aukerman, Miriam J. 1995. "Discrimination in Germany: A Call for Minority Rights." *Netherland Quarterly of Human Rights* 13: 237–57.

Baayen, Harald. 2008. *Analyzing Linguistic Data: A Practical Introduction to Statistics using R*. Cambridge: Cambridge University Press.

Baer, Susanne. 2005. *Report on Measures to Combat Discrimination Directives 2000/43/EC and 2000/78/EC, Country Report: Germany*. Brussels and Utrecht: Migration Policy Group and Human European Consultancy.

Ballmann, Alexander, David Epstein, and Sharyn O'Halloran. 2002. "Delegation, Comitology, and the Separation of Powers in the European Union." *International Organization* 56(3): 551–74.

Barber, Lionel. 1994. "Corfu may produce little more than fine snap-shots." *The Irish Times*, June 24, p. 8.

Baringhorst, Sigrid. 1995. "Symbolic Highlights or Political Enlightenment? Strategies for Fighting Racism in Germany." In *Racism, Ethnicity and Politics in Contemporary Europe*, ed. Alec G. Hargreaves and Jeremy Leaman. Aldershot: Edward Elgar, 225–39.

Barnard, Catherine. 1996. "The Economic Objectives of Article 119." In *Sex Equality Law of the European Union*, ed. Tamara K. Hervey and David O'Keefe. Hoboken, NJ: Wiley, 321–34.

—— 1997. "The United Kingdom, the 'Social Chapter' and the Amsterdam Treaty." *Industrial Law Journal* 26(3): 275–82.

BBC. 1999. "The Lawrence Inquiry." Available at <http://news.bbc.co.uk/2/hi/special_report/1999/02/99/stephen_lawrence/285357.stm>. Accessed November 11, 2013.

Begag, Azouz. 2007. *Ethnicity and Equality: France in the Balance*. Lincoln: University of Nebraska Press.

Bell, Mark. 1998. *EU Antidiscrimination Policy: From Equal Opportunities between Women and Men to Combating Racism*. Brussels: European Parliament Directorate General for Research.

—— 2000a. "The New Article 13 EC Treaty: A Platform for a European Policy against Racism." In *Race Discrimination: Developing and Using a New Legal Framework*, ed. Gay Moon. Oxford and Portland, OR: Hart Publishing, 81–112.

—— 2000b. "Article 13 EC: The European Commission's Anti-Discrimination Proposals." *Industrial Law Journal* 29(1): 79–84.

—— 2001. "Meeting the Challenge? A Comparison between the EU Racial Equality Directive and the Starting Line." In *The Starting Line and the Incorporation of the Racial Equality Directive into the National Laws of EU Member States and Accession States*, ed. Isabelle Chopin and Jan Niessen. London and Brussels: Commission for Racial Equality and Migration Policy Group, 22–54.

—— 2002. *Anti-Discrimination Law and the European Union*. Oxford: Oxford University Press.

—— 2007. "EU anti-racism policy; the leader of the pack?" In *Equality Law for an Enlarged Union: Understanding the Article 13 Directives*, ed. Helen Meenan. Cambridge: Cambridge University Press, 178–201.

—— 2008. *Racism and Equality in the European Union*. Oxford: Oxford University Press.

Black, Ian. 2000. "Austrian leader asks for a chance." *The Guardian* (London), March 9, p. 16.

Blatt, D. S. 1996. *Immigration Politics and Immigrant Collective Action in France, 1968–1993*. Ithaca: Cornell University Press.

Bleich, Eric. 2003. *Race Politics in Britain and France: Ideas and Policymaking since the 1960s*. Cambridge: Cambridge University Press.

Bleich, Eric and Mary Clare Feldmann. 2004. "The Rise of Race? Europeanization and Antiracist Policymaking in the EU." Paper presented at the conference The Impact of Europeanization on Politics and Policy in Europe: Trends and Trajectories, Toronto, University of Toronto, May 7–9.

Bonnett, Alastair. 1993. *Radicalism, Racism and Anti-Representation*. London: Routledge.

Börzel, Tanja A. 2000. "Why There Is no Southern Problem: On Environmental Leaders and Laggards in the European Union." *Journal of European Public Policy* 7(1): 141–62.

Bosch, Nicole and Mario Peucker. 2006. "National Data Collection Report 2005." *RAXEN 6 Report on Discrimination and Racism in Germany on behalf of the European Monitoring Centre on Racism and Xenophobia*. Bamberg: EUMC. Available at <http://www.efms.uni-bamberg.de/pdf/DE_2005_NDCR.pdf>. Accessed November 11, 2013.

Boučková, Pavla. 2009. "Report on Measures to Combat Discrimination: Directives 2000/43/EC and 2000/78/EC, Country Report 2009, Czech Republic. Utrecht, Brussels: European Network of Legal Experts in the Non-discrimination Field. Available at <http://www.non-discrimination.net/content/media/2009-CZ-Country%20Report%20LN_final.pdf>. Accessed November 17, 2013.

Boyce, D. George. 1999. *Decolonization and the British Empire*. New York: St. Martin's Press.

Brubaker, Rogers. 1992. *Citizenship and Nationhood in France and Germany*. Cambridge, MA: Harvard University Press.

Bündnis 90/Die Grünen. 2002: *Grün wirkt! Unser Wahlkampfprogramm 2002–2006*. Berlin: Bündnis 90/Die Grünen.

Button, James. 2005. "The Nowhere Generation: Europe's Year of Turmoil." *The Age*, December 31, p. 13.

Calvés, Gwenaele. 2002. "Il n'y pas de race ici: Le modele francaise a l'epreuve de l'integration europeene." *Critique Internationale* 17: 173–86.

Carter, Bob. 2000. *Realism and Racism: Concepts of Race in Sociological Research.* New York: Routledge.

Carvel, John. 1994. "EU plans action on racism." *The Guardian*, October 15, p. 14.

Chalmers, Damian. 2000a. "The Mistakes of the Good European?" *Queen's Papers on Europeanisation* No. 7/2000. Belfast: Queen's University.

——— 2000b. "The Positioning of EU Judicial Politics within the United Kingdom." *West European Politics* 23(4): 169–210.

Chopin, Isabelle. 1999a. *Article 13: A New Challenge for European Institutions.* Brussels: Migration Policy Group.

——— 1999b. *Campaigning against Racism and Xenophobia: From a Legislative Perspective at European Level.* Brussels: European Network against Racism.

——— 1999c. "The Starting Line Group: A Harmonised Approach to Fight Racism and to Promote Equal Treatment." *European Journal of Migration and Law* 1(1): 111–29.

——— 2000. "Harmonisation of Anti-Discrimination Legislation in the European Union: European and Non-Governmental Proposals." *European Journal of Migration and Law* 2(3–4): 413–43.

Chopin, Isabelle and Thien Uyen Do. 2011. *Developing Anti-Discrimination Law in Europe: The 27 EU Member States, Croatia, the Former Yugoslav Republic of Macedonia and Turkey Compared: November 2010.* Luxembourg: Publications Office of the European Union.

Chopin, Isabelle and Jan Niessen, eds. 1998. *Proposals for Legislative Measures to Combat Racism and to Promote Equal Rights in the European Union.* London and Brussels: Commission for Racial Equality and the Starting Line Group.

——— 2000. *Combating Racism in the European Union with Legal Means: A Comparison of the Starting Line with the EU Commission's Proposal for a Race Directive.* Brussels: Migration Policy Group.

——— eds. 2001. *The Starting Line and the Incorporation of the Racial Equality Directive into the National Law of EU Member States and Accession States.* London and Brussels: Commission for Racial Equality/Migration Policy Group.

——— eds. 2002. *Combating Racial and Ethnic Discrimination: Taking the Agenda Further.* London and Brussels: Commission for Racial Equality/Migration Policy Group.

Chopin, Isabelle, Janet Cormack, and Jan Niessen, eds. 2004. *The Implementation of European Anti-Discrimination Legislation: Work in Progress.* Brussels: Migration Policy Group.

Cichowski, Rachel A. 2007. *The European Court and Civil Society: Litigation, Mobilization and Governance.* Cambridge: Cambridge University Press.

Clüver, Cathryn. 2004. "Killing Me Softly: The Slow Death of Anti-Discrimination Legislation in Germany." *Challenge Europe Online Journal*, 14.

Cohen, Barbara. 2005. *Report on Measures to Combat Discrimination Directives 2000/43/EC and 2000/78/EC, Country Report: United Kingdom.* Belgium and Utrecht: Migration Policy Group and Human European Consultancy.

Conradt, David P. 2005. *The German Polity*, 8th edn. New York: Pearson Longman.

Cornelius, Wayne A., Philip L. Martin, and James F. Hollifield, eds. 1994. *Containing Immigration*. Palo Alto, CA: Stanford University Press.

Costa-Lascoux, J. 1994. "French Legislation against Racism." *New Community* 20(3): 371–79.

Cottle, Simon. 2004. *Media Performance and Public Transformation: The Racist Murder of Stephen Lawrence*. Westport, CT: Praeger.

—— 2005. "Mediatized Public Crisis and Civil Society Renewal: The Racist Murder of Stephen Lawrence." *Crime, Media, Culture* 1(1): 49–71.

Crowley, Niall. 2010. *Empty Promises: Bringing the Equality Authority to Heel*. Dublin: A. & A. Farmer.

Deutscher Gewerkschaftsbund Bildungswerk (DGB). 2006. "Entwurf eines Allgemeinen Gleichbehandlungsgesetzes soll die Schwächeren nachhaltig schützen." Available at <http://www.migration-online.de/data/gleichbehandlungsgesetz.pdf>. Accessed November 11, 2013.

Deutsche Presse-Agentur. 2000a. "EU executive notes 'inconsistencies' in Haider's comments," February 4.

—— 2000b. "Europeans promise tougher action on racism," February 24.

——2000c. "Get working on anti-discrimination package, says EU executive," March 13.

Dhume, Fabrice and Olivier Noel. 1999. "La discrimination raciale dans l'accès à l'emploi: un obstacle majeur à l'intégration et une place mineure dans le débat public." *Journal du Droit des Jeunes* 182: 40–42.

Diamantopoulou, Anna. 2003. "Commission concerned at Member States' failure to implement new racial equality rules." Opening address at Italian Presidency conference, Milan, July 18. Available at <http://europa.eu/rapid/press-release_IP-03-1047_en.pdf>. Accessed November 17, 2013.

Dobrushi, Andi. 2007. "Testing the Enforcement of Anti-Discrimination Laws in Europe: Selected ERRC Cases." In *Proceedings of the Seminar on the Racial Equality Directive Promoting Awareness of Community Rules against Racial Discrimination*, 83–96.

Doyle, Leonard. 1993. Unemployment and immigration in EC fuel right-wing extremism." *The Irish Times*, September 17, p. 17.

Duina, Francesco G. 1997. "Explaining Legal Implementation in the European Union." *International Journal of the Sociology of Law* 25(2): 155–79.

—— 1999. *Harmonizing Europe: Nation-States within the Common Market*. Albany: State University of New York Press.

Dummett, Ann. 1991. "Racial Equality and '1992.'" *Feminist Review* 39: 85–90.

—— 1994. "The Starting Line: A Proposal for a Draft Council Directive Concerning the Elimination of Racial Discrimination." *New Community* 20: 530–38.

Dupré, Catherine. 2003. *Importing the Law in Post-Communist Transitions: The Hungarian Court and the Right to Human Dignity*. Oxford and Portland, OR: Hart Publishing.

Durkheim, Émile. 1982. *The Rules of Sociological Method*. New York: Simon & Schuster.

Ebermeyer, Sophie. 2003. *Analytical Report on Housing*. October. Vienna: EUMC.

Eichener, V. 1993. *Social Dumping or Innovative Regulation? Processes and Outcomes of European Decision-Making in the Sector of Health and Safety at Work Harmonization*.

European University Institute Working Paper No. 92-28. Florence: European University Institute.

Engler, Marcus. 2007. "Länderprofil: Frankreich." Focus Migration. Berlin: Bundeszentrale für politische Bildung.

Europaforum. 1999. "Anti-Discrimination: The Way Forward: Article 13." Proceedings of the European Conference on Article 13, Vienna, December 1998. Ed. Eugen Antalovsky. Vienna: Europaforum.

European Commission. 1993. *Legal Instruments to Combat Racism and Xenophobia*. Luxembourg: Office for the Official Publications of the European Communities.

—— 1994. *European Social Policy—A Way Forward for the Union*. COM (94) 333 final, July 27.

—— 1997. *The European Institutions in the Fight against Racism: Selected Texts*. Luxembourg: Office for the Official Publications of the European Communities.

—— 2004. *Equal Rights in Practice: Key Voices 2004*. Luxembourg: Office for Official Publications of the European Union.

—— 2008. "Legal seminar in Brussels on the implementation of EU law on equal opportunities and anti-discrimination." Available at <http://ec.europa.eu/social/main.jsp?catId=88&langId=en&eventsId=132&furtherEvents=yes>. Accessed November 11, 2013.

European Commission against Racism and Intolerance (ECRI). 1995. "Legal Measures to Combat Racism and Intolerance in the Member States of the Council of Europe." Report prepared by the Swiss Institute of Comparative Law.

—— 1997. "Specialised bodies to combat racism, xenophobia, antisemitism and intolerance at national level." General Policy Recommendation No. 2, June 13.

——2010. "*ECRI Report on the United Kingdom: Fourth Monitoring Cycle.*" Strasbourg: Council of Europe, March 2.

European Council. 1995. *Final Report of the Consultative Commission on Racism and Xenophobia* [Kahn Report]. Brussels: 6906/1/95.

—— 2000. *Racial Equality Directive*: Council Directive 2000/43/EC. Brussels: Official Journal of the European Communities.

European Industrial Relations Observatory (EIRO). 2004 "Commission Launches Proceedings for Non-Implementation of Anti Discrimination Directives." Available at <http://www.eurofound.europa.eu/eiro/2004/08/inbrief/eu0408202n.htm>. Accessed November 11, 2013.

European Migration Network. 2010. "EMN Annual Policy Report 2009: National Contact Point of the Czech Republic to the European Migration Network." March.

European Network of Equality Bodies (Equinet). 2009. "Czech Republic pass anti-discrimination legislation." July 7.

European Parliament. 1985. *Committee of Inquiry into the Rise of Fascism and Racism in Europe* [Evrigenis Report]. Report on the Finding of the Inquiry.

—— 1991. *Report of the Findings: Committee of Inquiry on Racism and Xenophobia* [Ford Report]. Luxembourg: Office for Official Publications of the European Communities.

—— 1997. "European Union Anti-Discrimination Policy: From Equal Opportunities between Women and Men to Combatting Racism." Directorate-General for Research, Working document, Public Liberties Series (LIBE 102 EN). Available at

<http://www.europarl.europa.eu/workingpapers/libe/102/text1_en.htm#B_6_>. Accessed November 11, 2013.

European Union Agency for Fundamental Rights (FRA). 2009. Annual Report. Vienna: FRA.

—— 2009. *EU-MIDIS: European Union Minorities and Discrimination Survey*. Main Results Report. Vienna: FRA.

—— 2012. *The Racial Equality Directive: Application and Challenges*. Luxembourg: Publications Office of the European Union.

European Union Monitoring Centre on Racism and Xenophobia (EUMC). 2002. *Anti-Discrimination Legislation in EU Member States: A Comparison of National Anti-Discrimination Legislation on the Grounds of Racial or Ethnic Origin, Religion or Belief with Council Directives, the United Kingdom*. Vienna: EUMC.

—— 2010. *Legal Analysis of National and European Anti-Discrimination Legislation: A Comparison of the EU Racial Equality Directive & Protocol No. 12 with Anti-Discrimination Legislation*. Vienna: ERRC/Interights/MPG.

European Union Monitoring Centre on Racism and Xenophobia and Migration Policy Group (EUMC/MPG). 2000. *Research on National and European Legislation Combating Racism*. Luxembourg: Office for Official Publications of the European Communities.

Evans Case, Rhonda and Terri E. Givens. 2010. "Re-engineering Legal Opportunity Structures in the European Union? The Starting Line Group and the Politics of the Racial Equality Directive." *Journal of Common Market Studies* 48(2): 221–41.

Falkner, Gerda, Miriam Hartlapp, and Oliver Treib. 2007. "Worlds of Compliance: Why Leading Approaches to European Union Implementation are only 'Sometimes-True Theories.'" *European Journal of Political Research* 46(3): 395–416.

Falkner, Gerda, Oliver Treib, Miriam Hartlapp, and Simone Leiber. 2005. *Complying with Europe: EU Harmonization and Soft Law in the Member States*. Cambridge: Cambridge University Press.

Favell, Adrian. 1998. *Philosophies of Integration: Immigration and the Idea of Citizenship in France and Britain*. Basingstoke: Macmillan.

Fetzer, Joel S. and J. Christopher Soper. 2000. *Muslims and the State in Britain, France, and Germany*. Cambridge: Cambridge University Press.

Feuchtwanger, Edgar. 2001. *Imperial Germany 1850–1918*. London: Routledge.

Fifield, Dominic Hamelin. 2006. "We are Frenchmen says Thuram, as Le Pen bemoans number of black players." *Guardian*, June 30, p. 9.

Foner, Eric. 1990. *A Short History of Reconstruction 1863–1877*. New York: HarperCollins.

—— 2005. *In a New Land*. New York: New York University Press.

Ford, Glyn. 1992. *Fascist Europe: The Rise of Racism and Xenophobia*. Ann Arbor: University of Michigan Press.

Franchi, Vijé. *Analytical Report on Education*. Vienna: EUMC, 2004.

Freeman, Gary. 1979. *Immigrant Labor and Racial Conflict in Industrial Societies: The French and British Experience, 1945–1975*. Princeton, NJ: Princeton University Press.

French Ministry of Foreign Affairs. 2006a. "*La France á la loup*: Equal Opportunities Action in France." Available at <http://ambafrance-us.org/IMG/pdf/Equal_opportunities_action.pdf>. Accessed November 11, 2013.

—— 2006b. "*La France á la loup*: Measures taken after the suburban crisis in France." Available at <http://www.ambafrance-eau.org/IMG/suburban_crisis.pdf>. Accessed November 11, 2013.

Funk, Lothar. 2003. "Thematic feature—implementation of the EU framework equal treatment Directive, Germany." European Industrial Relations Observatory Online. Available at <http://www.eurofound.europa.eu/eiro/2003/08/tfeature/de0308101t. htm>. Accessed November 11, 2013.

Gearty, Conor A. 1999. "The Internal and External 'Other' in the Union Legal Order: Racism, Religious Intolerance and Xenophobia in Europe." In *The EU and Human Rights*, ed. Philip Alston. Oxford: Oxford University Press, 327–58.

Geddes, Andrew. 2000. "Lobbying for Migrant Inclusion in the European Union: New Opportunities for Transnational Advocacy?" *Journal of European Public Policy* 7(4): 632–49.

—— 2003a. "Integrating Immigrants and Minorities in a Wider and Deeper Europe." In *Europeanization, National Identities and Migration: Changes in Boundary Constructions between Western and Eastern Europe*, ed. Willfried Spohn and Anna Triandafyllidou. London: Routledge, 83–98.

—— 2003b. *The Politics of Migration and Immigration in Europe*. New York: Sage.

Geddes, Andrew and Virginie Guiraudon. 2002. "Anti-Discrimination Policy: The Emergence of an EU Policy Paradigm amidst Contrasted National Models." Paper presented at the workshop Opening the Black Box: Europeanisation, Discourse, and Policy Change. Oxford, November 23–24.

—— 2004. "Britain, France, and EU Anti-Discrimination Policy: The Emergence of an EU Policy Paradigm." *West European Politics* 27: 334–55.

—— 2007. "The Europeanization of Anti-Discrimination in Britain and France." In *European Anti-Discrimination and the Politics of Citizenship: Britain and France*, ed. Christophe Bertossi. Basingstoke: Palgrave Macmillan, 125–42.

"German Jews tell Kohl of racism worries." 1994. *The Jerusalem Post*, May 3, p. 4.

"Germany: Citizenship, Asylum." 1998. *Migration News* 4(4). Available at <http://migration.ucdavis.edu/mn/more.php?id=3461_0_4_0>. Accessed November 11, 2013.

Gilroy, Paul. 1990. "One Nation Under a Groove: The Cultural Politics of 'Race' and Racism in Britain." In *Anatomy of Racism*, ed. David Theo Goldberg. Minneapolis: University of Minnesota Press, 263–82.

Givens, Terri E. 2005. *Voting Radical Right in Western Europe*. Cambridge: Cambridge University Press.

Givens, Terri E. and A. Luedtke. 2004. "The Politics of European Union Immigration Policy: Institutions, Salience, and Harmonization." *Policy Studies Journal* 32(1): 145–65.

Glendon, Mary Ann. 1991. *Rights Talk: The Impoverishment of Political Discourse*. New York: Free Press.

Green, Simon. 2004. *The Politics of Exclusion: Institutions and Immigration Policy in Contemporary Germany*. Manchester: Manchester University Press.

Griller, Stefan, Dimitri P. Droutsas, Gerda Falkner, Katrin Forgó, and Michael Nentwich. 2000. *The Treaty of Amsterdam: Facts, Analysis, Prospects*. New York: Springer-Verlag.

Grimmer, Justin. 2010. "A Bayesian Hierarchical Topic Model for Political Texts: Measuring Expressed Agendas in Senate Press Releases." *Political Analysis* 18: 1–35.

Groenendijk, Kees. 1999. "Why a New Journal on Migration and Law?" *European Journal of Migration & Law* 1: 1–7.

—— 2004. "Legal Concepts and the Integration of the EU." *European Journal of Migration and Law* 6: 111–26.

Guild, Elspeth. 2000. "European Developments: The EC Directive on Race Discrimination: Surprises, Possibilities and Limitations." *Industrial Law Journal* 29: 416–42.

—— 2001. "The European Union and Article 13 of the Treaty Establishing the European Community." In *Race Discrimination: Developing and Using a New Legal Framework*, ed. Gay Moon. Oxford and Portland, OR: Hart Publishing, 65–79.

Guiraudon, Virginie. 1999. "European Integration and Migration Policy: The Implications of Vertical Policy-Making." Paper presented at the meeting of the European Studies Association, Pittsburgh, PA. Available at <http://aei.pitt.edu/2281/01/002341_1.PDF>. Accessed November 11, 2013.

—— 2000. *Les politiques d'immigration en Europe: Allemagne, France, Pays-Bas.* Paris: L'Harmattan.

—— 2001. "Weak Weapons of the Weak? Transnational Mobilization around Migration in the European Union." In *Contentious Europeans: Protest and Politics in an Emerging Polity*, ed. Doug Imig and Sydney Tarrow. Lanham, MD: Rowman & Littlefield, 163–84.

—— 2004. "Construire une politique européenne de lutte contre les discriminations." *Sociétés contemporaines* 53: 11–32.

Haas, Ernst. 1958. *The Uniting of Europe*. Stanford: Stanford University Press.

—— 1992. "Introduction: Epistemic Communities and International Policy Coordination." *International Organization* 46(1): 1–35.

Hall, Peter. 1993. "Policy Paradigms, Social Learning and the State: The Case of Economic Policy-Making in Britain." *Comparative Politics* 25: 275–96.

Hall, Peter A. and Rosemary C. R. Taylor. 1996. "Political Science and the Three New Institutionalisms." *Political Studies* 44: 936–57.

Hall, Stuart. 1999. "From Scarman to Stephen Lawrence." *History Workshop Journal* 48: 187–97.

Hammer, U. and U. Rzadkowski. 1991. "Antidiskriminierungsgesetz für homosexuelle Frauen und Männer in Arbeit und Beruf." *Zeitschrift für Tarifrecht Heft* 9/1991.

Hansen, Randall. 2000. *Citizenship and Immigration in Post-War Britain: The Institutional Origins of a Multicultural Nation*. Oxford: Oxford University Press.

Hargreaves, Alec G. 1995. *Immigration, 'Race' and Ethnicity in Contemporary France*. London: Routledge.

Haverland, Markus. 2000. "National Adaptation to the European Integration: The Importance of Institutional Veto Points." *Journal of Public Policy* 20: 83–103.

Heckmann, Friedrich and Dominique Schnapper, eds. 2003. *The Integration of Immigrants in European Societies: National Differences and Trends in Convergence.* Stuttgart: Lucius & Lucius.

Heritier, Adrienne et al. 2001. *Differential Europe: EU Impact on National Policymaking.* Lanham, MD: Rowman & Littlefield.

Hermanin, Costanza. 2012. "Europeanization through Judicial Rule-Making? The Case of Race Equality." Paper presented at the Jean Monnet Workshop on EU Antidiscrimination Law and Policy, Temple University, Philadelphia, PA, April 13.

Hieronymus, Andreas and Meena Moses. 2002. *Talking "Race" in Germany*. ENAR Schattenbericht Deutschland. Brussels: European Network Against Racism.

Hix, Simon and Jan Niessen. 1996. *Reconsidering European Migration Policies: The 1996 IGC and the Reform of the Maastricht Treaty.* Washington, DC and Brussels: Migration Policy Group.

Holtmaat, Rikki. 2006. *Catalysts for Change? Equality bodies according to Directive* 2000/43/EC, MPG, HEC, European Commission. Available at <http://www.migpolgroup.org/public/docs/11.CatalystsforChange_Equality BodiesaccordingtoDir2000.43.EC_EN_03.06.pdf>. Accessed November 11, 2013.

Hönekopp, Elmar (IAB), Gisela Will, and Stefan Rühl. 2002. *Migrants, Minorities and Employment in the United Kingdom: Exclusion, Discrimination and Anti-Discrimination.* RAXEN 3, Report to the EUMC. London: EUMC.

Hooghe, Liesbet and Gary Marks. 2001. *Multi-Level Governance and European Integration.* Lanham, MD: Rowman & Littlefield.

Hoskyns, Catherine. 1986. "Women, European Law and Transnational Politics." *International Journal of the Sociology of Law* 14: 299–315.

Howard, Marc Morjé. 2009. *The Politics of Citizenship in Europe.* Cambridge: Cambridge University Press.

Hussain, Asifa Maaria. 2001. *British Immigration Policy under the Conservative Government.* Burlington, VT: Ashgate.

Hutchings, Vincent L. and Nicholas A. Valentino. 2004. "The Centrality of Race in American Politics." *Annual Review of Political Science* 7: 383–408.

Hutchinson, Tansy. 2007. "The Race Equality Directive: The Role of NGOS." Paper presented at the Seminar on the Racial Equality Directive Promoting Awareness of Community Rules against Racial Discrimination, Istanbul, June 25–26.

Immergut, Ellen M. 1992. *Health Politics: Interests and Institutions in Western Europe.* Cambridge: Cambridge University Press.

Institut National d'Etudes Démographiques (INED) and Institut National de la Statistique et des Etudes Economiques (INSEE). 1992–93. *"L'enquête Mobilité géographique et insertion sociale.* Paris: INED-INSEE.

Interights. 2003. *Annual Review 2002–2003.* London: Interights.

Interights, ERRC, and MPG. 2004. *Strategic Litigation of Race Discrimination in Europe: From Principles to Practice.* Brussels, Budapest, and London: Interrights, European Roma Rights Center, and Migration Policy Group.

Ireland, Patrick. 2004. *Becoming Europe: Immigration, Integration, and the Welfare State.* Pittsburgh: University of Pittsburgh Press.

Isensee, J. 1974. "Die staatsrechliche Stellung der Ausländer in der Bundesrepublik Deutschland." *Veröffentlichungen der Vereinigung der Deutschen Staatsrechtslehrer (VVDStRL)* 32: 49–101.

Joppke, Christian. 1999. *Immigration and the Nation-State.* Oxford: Oxford University Press.

—— 2007. "Transformation of Immigrant Integration: Civic Integration and Antidiscrimination in the Netherlands, France, and Germany." *World Politics* 59: 243–73.

Karatani, Rieko. 2003. *Defining British Citizenship: Empire, Commonwealth and Modern Britain.* New York: Routledge.

Katznelson, Ira. 1973. *Black Men, White Cities: Race, Politics, and Migration in the United States and Britain, 1948–69.* Chicago: University of Chicago Press.

—— 1987. *Policy & Politics West Germany: The Growth of a Semisovereign State.* Philadelphia: Temple University Press.

Keck, Margaret and Kathryn Sikkink. 1998. *Activists beyond Borders.* Ithaca: Cornell University Press.

—— 1999. "Transnational Advocacy Networks in International and Regional Politics." *International Social Science Journal* 51: 89–101.

Kitschelt, Herbert. 1995. *The Radical Right in Western Europe.* Ann Arbor: University of Michigan Press.

Klimas, Tadas and Jurate Vaiciukaite. 2008. "The Law of Recitals in European Community Legislation." *ILSA Journal of International & Comparative Law,* 15. Available at <http://ssrn.com/abstract=1159604>. Accessed November 11, 2013.

Knill, Christoph and Andrea Lenschow. 1998. "Coping with Europe: The Impact of British and German Administrations on the Implementation of EU Environmental Policy." *Journal of European Public Policy* 5(4): 595–614.

König, Thomas and Thomas Bräuninger. 1997. "Wie wichtig sind die *Länder* in der Einspruchs- und Zustimmungsgesetzgebung?" *Zeitschrift für Parlamentsfragen* 28: 605–28.

Koopmans, Ruud. 1999. "Political. Opportunity. Structure. Some Splitting to Balance the Lumping." *Sociological Forum* 14(1): 93–105.

Kretzschmar, Cyril, Sophie Ebermeyer, and Mathieu Dehoumon. 2004. Résumé analytique de la directive de l'égalité de traitement sans distinction de race, Etat actuel en France. Available at <http://europa.eu.int/comm/employment_social/ fundamental_rights/pdf/legisln/msracequality/france.pdf>. Accessed November 3, 2004.

Ladeur, Karl-Heinz. 2002. "Private Law The German Proposal of an 'Anti-Discrimination' Law: Anticonstitutional and Anti-Common Sense. A Response to Nicola Vennemann." *German Law Journal* 3(5). Available at <http://www.ger manlawjournal.com/article.php?id=152>. Accessed November 11, 2013.

Laflache, Michelynn. 1998. "Network Objectives Achieved." *The Runnymede Bulletin* 309: 5. Available at <http://www.runnymedetrust.org/uploads/publications/ pdfs/1998February.pdf>. Accessed November 11, 2013.

Lahav, Gallya. 2004. *Immigration and Politics in the New Europe: Reinventing Borders.* Cambridge: Cambridge University Press.

Latraverse, Sophie. 2007. *Report on Measures to Combat Discrimination Directives 2000/43/EC and 2000/78/EC, Country Report: France: State of affairs up to 8 January 2007.* Belgium and Utrecht: Migration Policy Group and Human European Consultancy.

Lavenex, Sandra. 2006. "Towards the Constitutionalization of Aliens' Rights in the European Union?" *Journal of European Public Policy* 13(8): 1284–1301.

Layton-Henry, Zig. 1984. *The Politics of Race in Britain.* London: Allen & Unwin.

—— 1992. *The Politics of Immigration: Race and Race Relations in Postwar Britain.* London: Wiley-Blackwell.

Leitner, Helga. 1997. "Reconfiguring the Spatiality of Power: The Construction of a Supra-National Migration Framework for the European Union." *Political Geography* 16(2): 123–43.

Lichbach, Mark. 2003. *Is Rational Choice Theory All of Social Science?* Ann Arbor: University of Michigan Press.

Lieberman, Robert C. 2005. *Shaping Race Policy: The United States in Comparative Perspective.* Princeton, NJ: Princeton University Press.

Lindberg, Leon. 1963. *The Political Dynamics of European Economic Integration.* Stanford: Stanford University Press.

Lloyd, T. O. 1984. *The British Empire 1558–1983.* Oxford: Oxford University Press.

Lutz, Ellen and Kathryn Sikkink. 2001. "The Justice Cascade: The Evolution and Impact of Foreign Human Rights Trials in Latin America." *Chicago Journal of International Law* 2(1): 1–33.

Mahlmann, Matthias. 2002. "Germany. Anti-Discrimination Legislation in EU Member States: A Comparison of National Anti-Discrimination Legislation on the Grounds of Racial or Ethnic Origin, Religion or Belief with the Council Directives." Vienna: European Monitoring Centre on Racism and Xenophobia. Available at <http://www.pedz.uni-mannheim.de/daten/edz-b/ebr/02/ART13_Germany-en.pdf>. Accessed November 11, 2013.

Marlowe, Lara. 2001. "French racism law needs changing, says group." *The Irish Times,* February 12, p. 5.

Matsuda, Mari J. and Charles R. Lawrence III. 1993. *Words that Wound: Critical Race Theory, Assaultive Speech, and the First Amendment.* Boulder, CO: Westview Press.

Mehta, Jal. 2011. "The Varied Roles of Ideas in Politics: From 'Whether' to 'How.'" In *Ideas and Politics in Social Science Research,* ed. Daniel Béland and Robert Henry Cox. New York: Oxford University Press, 23–46.

Messina, Anthony M. 2007. *The Logics and Politics of Post-WWII Migration to Western Europe.* New York: Cambridge University Press.

Metcalf, Thomas R. 1997. *Ideologies of the Raj.* Cambridge: Cambridge University Press.

Miller, Mark J. 2002. "Continuity and Change in Postwar French Legalization Policy." In *West European Immigration and Immigrant Policy in the New Century,* ed. Anthony M. Messina. Westport, CT: Praeger Publishers, 13–32.

Modood, Tariq. 2005. *Multicultural Politics: Racism, Ethnicity, and Muslims in Britain.* Minneapolis: University of Minnesota Press.

Moe, Terry. 1984. "The New Economics of Organization." *American Journal of Political Science* 28: 739–77.

—— 1990. "The Politics of Structural Choice: Toward a Theory of Public Bureaucracy." In *Organization Theory: From Chester Barnard to the Present and Beyond,* ed. O. E. Williamson. Oxford: Oxford University Press, 116–53.

Money, Jeannette. 1999. *Fences and Neighbors: The Political Geography of Immigration Control.* Ithaca: Cornell University Press.

Moravscik, Andrew. 1993. "Preferences and Power in the European Community." *Journal of Common Market Studies* 31(4): 473–524.

—— 1997. "Taking Preferences Seriously: A Liberal Theory of International Politics." *International Organization* 51(4): 512–53.

—— 1998. *The Choice for Europe: Social Purpose and State Power from Messina to Maastricht.* Ithaca: Cornell University Press.

Mudde, Cas. 2007. *Populist Radical Right Parties in Europe.* Cambridge: Cambridge University Press.

Murphy, Kara. 2006. "France's New Law: Control Immigration Flows, Court the Highly Skilled." MPI website. Available at <http://www.migrationpolicy.org/pubs/Backgrounder2_France.php>. Accessed November 11, 2013.

Neuendorf, Kimberly. 2002. *The Content Analysis Guidebook*. Thousand Oaks: Sage Publications.

Nickel, Rainer. 1996. *Rechtlicher Schutz gegen Diskriminierung—Ein Leitfaden*. Frankfurt am Main: Fachhochschulverlag.

Niessen, Jan. 2000a. "The Amsterdam Treaty and NGO Responses." *European Journal of Migration and Law* 2: 203–14.

—— 2000b. "The Starting Line and the Promotion of EU Anti-Discrimination Legislation: The Role of Policy Oriented Research." *Journal of International Migration and Integration* 1(4): 493–503.

—— 2003. "Making the Law Work: The Enforcement and Implementation of Anti-Discrimination Legislation." *European Journal of Migration and Law* 5: 249–57.

Niessen, Jan and Isabelle Chopin, eds. 2004. *The Development of Legal Instruments to Combat Racism in a Diverse Europe*. Leiden: Martinus Nijhoff Publishers.

Norris, P. 2005. *Radical Right: Parties and Electoral Competition*. Cambridge: Cambridge University Press.

Oezcan, Veysel. 2004. "Germany: Immigration in Transition." MPI website. Available at <http://www.migrationinformation.org/Profiles/display.cfm?ID=235>. Accessed November 11, 2013.

Organisation for Economic Co-operation and Development (OECD). 2006. *International Migration Outlook*. Paris: SOPEM.

Peters, B. G. 1992. "Bureaucratic Politics and the Institutions of the European Community." In *Europolitics: Institutions and Policymaking in the "New" European Community*, ed. A. Sbragia. Washington, DC: Brookings Institution, 75–122.

Pettigrew, Thomas F. 1998. "Reactions toward the New Minorities of Western Europe." *Annual Review of Sociology* 24: 77–103.

Pierson, Paul. 1996. "The Path to European Integration: A Historical Institutionalist Analysis." *Comparative Political Studies* 29(2): 123–63.

—— 2003. *Politics in Time: History, Institutions, and Social Analysis*. Princeton, NJ: Princeton University Press.

—— 2004. *Politics in Time*. Princeton, NJ: Princeton University Press.

Pierson, Paul and Theda Skocpol. 2000. "Historical Institutionalism in Contemporary Political Science." Paper presented at the American Political Science Association annual meeting, Washington DC, September.

Pulzer, Peter. 2003. "The Devil They Know: The German Federal Election of 2002." *West European Politics* 26(2): 153–64.

Quillian, Lincoln. 1995. "Prejudice as a Response to Perceived Group Threat." *American Sociological Review* 60: 586–611.

Quinn, Frederick. 2000. *The French Overseas Empire*. Westport, CT: Praeger.

Radcliffe, P. 2001. " 'Ethnic Group' and the Population Census in Great Britain: Mission Impossible?" *Mesure et Malmesure des Populations*. Paris: CERI and INED.

Recht, Sophie. 2002. "France." In *Anti-Discrimination Legislation in EU Member States: A Comparison of National Anti-Discrimination Legislation on the Grounds of Racial or Ethnic Origin, Religion or Belief with the Council Directives*, ed. Jan Niessen and Isabelle Chopin. Vienna: European Monitoring Centre on Racism and Xenophobia. Available at <http://www.pedz.uni-mannheim.de/daten/edz-b/ebr/02/ART13_France-en.pdf>. Accessed November 11, 2013.

Risse, Thomas, Maria Green Cowles, and James Caporaso. 2001. "Europeanization and Domestic Change: Introduction," in *Transforming Europe: Europeanization and Domestic Change*, ed. Maria Green Cowles, James Caporaso, and Thomas Risse. Ithaca: Cornell University Press, 1–20.

Rorive, Isabelle. 2009. *Proving Discrimination Cases: The Role of Situation Testing*. Brussels and Stockholm: Migration Policy Group and Centre for Equal Rights.

Rosenberg, Clifford. 2006. *Policing Paris*. Ithaca: Cornell University Press.

Rutherford, Andrew. 2011. *ANOVA and ANCOVA: A GLM approach*. Hoboken, NJ: Wiley.

Ruzza, Carlo. 1999. "Anti-Racism and EU Institutions." Paper presented at the European Sociological Association Conference, Amsterdam, Netherlands, August 18–21.

Schattschneider, Elmer E. 1960. *The Semisovereign People: A Realist's View of Democracy in America*. San Diego, CA: Harcourt.

Schmidt, Vivien. 2008. "Discursive Institutionalism: The Explanatory Power of Ideas and Discourse." *Annual Review of Political Science* 11: 303–26.

—— 2011. "Reconciling Ideas and Institutions." In *Ideas and Politics in Social Science Research*, ed. Daniel Béland and Robert Henry Cox. New York: Oxford University Press, 47–64.

Schnapper, Dominique, Pascale Krief, and Emmanuel Peignard. 2003. "French Immigration and Integration Policy: A Complex Combination." In *The Integration of Immigrants in European Societies: National Differences and Trends in Convergence*, ed. Friedrich Heckman and Dominique Schnapper. Stuttgart: Lucius and Lucius, 15–44.

Schwerdtfeger, G. 1980. "Welche rechtliche Vorkehrungen empfehlen sich, um die Rechtstellung von Ausländern in der Bundesrepublik Deutschland angemessen zu gestalten?" In *Verhandlungen des Dreiundfünfzigsten deutschen Juristentags Berlin 1980*, Vol. II. Munich: Beck, Gutachten A: A 119.

Shachar, Ayelet. 2006. "The Race for Talent: Highly Skilled Migrants and Competitive Immigration Regimes." *New York University Law Review* 81(1): 148–206.

Shapiro, Martin and Alec Stone Sweet. 2002. *On Law, Politics, and Judicialization*. Oxford: Oxford University Press.

Simmons, Harvey. 1996. *The French National Front: The Extremist Challenge to Democracy*. Boulder, CO: Westview Press.

Skocpol, Theda. 1995. "Why I Am a Historical Institutionalist." *Polity* 28(1): 103–6.

Small, Stephen and John Solomos. 2006. "Race, Immigration and Politics in Britain." *International Journal of Comparative Sociology* 47(3–4): 235–57.

Sommerville, Will. 2007. "The Immigration Legacy of Tony Blair." Migration Policy Institute. Available at <http://www.migrationinformation.org/Feature/display.cfm?ID=600>. Accessed November 11, 2013.

Stacey, Jeffrey. 2010. *Integrating Europe: Informal Politics & Institutional Change*. Oxford: Oxford University Press.

Staunton, Denis. 2000. "Haider sparks off fresh controversy by accusing Turks of refusing to integrate Austria's new government is snubbed at Lisbon meeting." *The Irish Times*, February 12, p. 15.

Stephen Lawrence Inquiry. 1999. *Report of an Inquiry by Sir William MacPherson of Cluny*, Cm 3684. London: HMSO.

Tikly, Leon. 2004. *Analytical Report on Education*. Vienna: EUMC.

Tilly, Charles. 1978. *From Mobilization to Revolution*. New York: Longman Higher Education.

Treaty of Amsterdam. 1997. Available at <http://www.eurotreaties.com/amsterdamtreaty.pdf>. Accessed November 11, 2013.

Tsebelis, George. 1994. "The Power of the European Parliament as a Conditional Agenda Setter." *American Political Science Review* 88(1): 128–42.

—— 1995. "Decision Making in Poitical Systems: Veto Players in Presidentialism, Parliamentarianism, Multicameralism and Multipartyism." *British Journal of Political Science* 25: 289–326.

—— 2002. *Veto Players: How Political Institutions Work*. Princeton, NJ: Princeton University Press.

Tyson, Adam. 2001. "The Negotiation of the EC Directive on Racial Discrimination." *European Journal of Migration and Law* 3(2): 199–229.

United Nations. 1949. "The main types and causes of discrimination; memorandum submitted by the Secretary-General." Lake Success: United Nations, Commission on Human Rights, Sub-commission on the Prevention of Discrimination and Protection of Minorities. Series: E/CN.4/Sub.2/40/rev. 1. 7, June.

Verbunt, G. 1985. *European Immigration Policy: A Comparative Study*. Cambridge: Cambridge University Press.

Wallace, Adrienne. 2000. "The Development of an Anti-Race Discrimination Policy in the European Union." PhD Dissertation, Department of Politics, New York University.

Weiler, J. H. H. 1986. "Eurocracy and Distrust." *Washington Law Review* 61: 1103–42.

Whalen, Charles and Barbara Whalen. 1985. *The Longest Debate: A Legislative History of the 1964 Civil Rights Act*. Washington, DC: Seven Locks.

Whittle, R. 1998. "Disability Discrimination and the Amsterdam Treaty." *European Law Review* 27(3): 303–26.

Will, Gisela. 2003. *Analytical Report on Housing*. October. Vienna: EUMC.

Will, Gisela and Stefan Rühl. 2004a. *Analytical Report on Education*. Vienna: EUMC.

—— 2004b. *Analytical Report on Legislation*. Vienna: EUMC.

Wilpert, Czarina. 2003. "Germany: From Workers to Entrepreneurs." In *Immigrant Entrepreneurs: Venturing Abroad in the Age of Globalization*, ed. Robert Kloosterman and Jan Rath. Oxford and New York: Berg Publishers, 233–60.

Wisskirchen, Gerland and Christopher Jordan. 2004. "Development of Anti-Discrimination and Anti-Sexual Harassment Law in Germany and in the EU." American Bar Association. Available at <http://www.bna.com/bnabooks/ababna/annual/2004/wisskirchen.doc>. Accessed May 2, 2009.

Won-Pil Suh, Raphael and Richard Bales. 2006. "German and European Employment Discrimination Policy." *Oregon Review of International Law* 8: 263–306.

Wright, Michelle. 2004. *Becoming Black: Creating Identity in the African Diaspora*. Duham, NC: Duke University Press.

Young, C. 1983. "The Temple of Ethnicity." *World Politics* 35(4): 652–62.

Yu, Patrick. 2006. "The Role of NGOs in Europe: The Experience of NICEM." *Brussels Bulletin* 9: 15–16.

Yu, Patrick and Isaabelle Chopin. 2001. "Introduction." In *The Starting Line and the Incorporation of the Racial Equality Directive into the National Laws of the EU*

Member States and Accession States, ed. Isabelle Chopin and Jan Niessen. London and Brussels: Commission for Racial Equality/Migration Policy Group, 5–6.

Zolberg, Aristide R. 2006. "Patterns of International Migration Policy: A Diachronic Comparison." In *The Migration Reader*, ed. Anthony M. Messina and Gallya Lahav. Boulder, CO: Lynne Rienner, 63–89.

Zypries, Brigitte. 2003a. "Vortrag Bundesministerin Zypries—Kammerversammlung des OLG Celle." Available at <http://www.bmj.bund.de>.

—— 2003b. "Rede Bundesjustizministerin—Zentralverbandstag der Deutschen Haus-, Wohnungs- und Grundeigentümer." Available at <http://www.bmj.bund.de>.

—— 2004. "Bundesjustizministerin Zipries: Diskriminierungsschutz mit Augenmaß." Available at <http://www.bmj.bund.de>.

Index